Following Jesus

Dyron Daughrity

An Imprint of Sulis International Press
Los Angeles | Dallas | London

FOLLOWING JESUS
Copyright ©2025 by Dyron Daughrity. All rights reserved.

No part of this book may be reproduced in any form or by any means without the prior written consent of the Publisher, excepting brief quotes used in reviews.

ISBN: 978-1-958139-73-8

Published by Keledei Publications
An Imprint of Sulis International
Los Angeles | Dallas | London

www.sulisinternational.com

Other Keledei Publications Books by Dyron Daughrity

How the Book of James Teaches Us To Be True Disciples of Jesus (2023).

Live Holy and Godly Lives (2024)

Joy in the Morning (2025)

Contents

1. Put the Focus on God 1
2. We Are Not of this World 11
3. Choosing Your Team..21
4. Live a Humble Life 29
5. How to Deal with the Ahabs and Jezebels.............37
6. God's Providential Protection 47
7. The Power of Perception 55
8. The Tale of Two Chameleons..................................65
9. Elevate the People Around You 75
10. Love: The Heart of Christianity 83
11. The Problem with Secrets 93
12. Go Out and Spread the Good News 101
13. God and Mammon..109
14. Jesus Taught Us to Pray......................................119
15. Listen, With Empathy...127
16. When to take other opinions seriously 135
17. Neither Do I Condemn You 143
18. Therefore, Keep Watch 151
19. How to mess up your life: Be Selfish..................161
20. "Follow Me," Declares the Lord..........................169

1. Put the Focus on God

This book's intention is simple: to encourage Christians to refocus our attention on the source of our faith: Jesus Christ. Our main duty in life is to obey Him, please Him, lift Him up, love Him, share Him, and, of course, "Follow Him."

In life, we have a choice of who or what we're going to follow. My kids and I recently had a conversation about "heroes." It is a difficult concept because we need heroes. We long for them. We love to watch movies with a hero saving the world in it. We need a protagonist. We need icons. We need people that inspire us and make us want to emulate them. I need them and so do you. And to an extent, it is healthy to have people we admire and look up to. However, we must know that our heroes are very, very limited. They will let us down, eventually. That's why they say you should "never meet your heroes!"

The other mistake that some people make is that they follow their own desires. They get obsessed with themselves. They put themselves first in everything. This is wrongheaded, but it can also become dangerous because we will definitely let ourselves down! I don't think any of us are heroic to ourselves! I am the first person to realize how un-iconic I am! I can say with confidence: don't "pedestalize" me! Please! I'm a sinner. I try, but I will definitely let you down if you are around me long enough.

And we're all like this. We're so imperfect. We're flawed. We're lost without direction. And we need someone or something to follow.

We live in a self-obsessed world. We have "influencers," we have social media all around us, we have a culture where people are clamoring for attention.

Remember that word that entered the English lexicon several years ago? "Selfie." That word says a lot about our society. At its base, it is an entirely selfish concept—you simply take a picture of yourself. Many of us are prone to take selfies, but the practice can get out of hand ... as it did in India back in 2016.

It was in the megacity of Mumbai, formerly known as Bombay. There was a series of selfie accidents that were completely unnecessary. In order to deal with the problem of people accidentally killing themselves while doing selfies, they established 16 "no selfie zones."

The United States has had similar problems. The *Washington Post* reported that over 250 people died in recent years while attempting to take selfies. People have drowned during selfies (actually the #1 cause of selfie deaths), they have fallen out of vehicles or crashed, they have fallen from high places such as the Grand Canyon and high elevation hotels, they have posed for selfies with wild animals that killed them, and they have accidentally electrocuted themselves.

What is going on here? Why did all of this happen?

Sociologically speaking, what caused this massive sea change in how we conduct ourselves? Why would you endanger your life just to get a picture of yourself doing something dangerous? Do we want people to think we're dangerous? Is it really cool to be dangerous? We should probably count the cost, and realize that if we are that focused on impressing people in our social networks, then we've obviously got more serious problems.

I remember when I was a kid, once in a very long while I would ask someone to take a picture of me ... but the vast majority of my photos were of trees, my pets, my friends, beautiful landscapes, and perhaps cool-looking cars. Now days, people still take pictures of all that stuff, but they want their own face in it. What caused this shift? I don't recall wanting my face in the picture when photographing a beautiful, cherry-red Mustang convertible.

I think part of this shift has to do with the fact that the cell-phone made it so easy to take pictures and share them. Secondly, I suspect a lot of it is simply peer pressure. We do it because everyone else is doing it. However, that doesn't answer the core question: Why did this begin at all? Could it be that we have become far more self-centered than we used to be?

While I do think we have allowed our selfishness to go to a whole new level in recent years, the Bible makes it clear that "me-centered thinking" has been around for a long time. I am reminded of Jesus's Sermon on the Mount, in Matthew 6:1, where he says, "Be careful not to practice your righteousness in front of others to be seen by them. If you do, you will have no reward from your Father in heaven."

In that same chapter, Jesus tells his hearers the following (Matthew 6:2-4):

> So when you give to the needy, do not announce it with trumpets, as the hypocrites do in the synagogues and on the streets, to be honored by others. Truly I tell you, they have received their reward in full. But when you give to the needy, do not let your left hand know what your right hand is doing so that your giving may be in secret. Then your Father, who sees what is done in secret, will reward you.

Then Jesus says (Matthew 6:5-6):

> And when you pray, do not be like the hypocrites, for they love to pray standing in the synagogues and on the street corners to be seen by others. Truly I tell you, they have received their reward in full. But when you pray, go into your room, close the door and pray to your Father, who is unseen. Then your Father, who sees what is done in secret, will reward you.

I think there are two major lessons here. The first is that God doesn't like it when people simply follow Him for show. He warns against it directly. People who do this kind of thing are called hypocrites. Their religion is all messed up. It is about "me." They simply want to be exalted. They want to be praised. They want glory for themselves, when in fact all glory should be given to God, not to us.

But the second major issue here has to do with intimacy with God. Our relationship with God is not for show. It is not for social media. It is not for public viewing. Sure, if someone notices that we pray before taking our meals in a restaurant, then that's well and good. If someone notices you posting a Bible passage on YouVersion, then that's well and good.

But we must get this straight right here. Our public image is not supposed to come first. If our religiosity or piety becomes known to someone, that's fine. Our relationship with Jesus, however, is to be deep and private. We are to love Jesus in our hearts, pray to Him in secret, and love him in our minds.

As a preaching minister, I have to struggle with this because I am called to preach the Word publicly. So, there are times I use analogies from my private life in order to make a point. And I feel torn about this sometimes. But I hope you will always keep it in perspective that my relationship with God is not something that is first of all public and second of all private. I try real hard to keep it straight: my faith must first of all be a private, deeply intimate thing with Jesus. And secondly, it kind of plays out in my public ministry.

There is nothing quite like taking a long walk with the Lord. Talking with Him. Being with Him. Just sitting and thinking about Him. Reaching out to Him. It is vital that we, as Christ-followers, get out there in nature, or in a park, or even on the sidewalks of our local neighborhood, and just pray to God. Thank him for all he's done for you in your life. Ask him to be with you as you travel your life's pathway. Ask him to bless your family and friends. Pray for people, by name, so that they might be okay. Mention their name, so that the power of heaven will be released upon them, personally. God will hear your prayer. He will give attention to the people you are mentioning before the Throne of Grace.

Being a Christian means that we develop intimacy with God. That is not a public thing. It is an intensely private thing. And it is so rewarding. We all feel like hypocrites, don't we, when we go to church and fellowship and sing, but then in our hearts sometimes we realize we have not been behaving like Christians in our personal life.

But when you are getting more deeply rooted in your faith, praying privately, reading scripture quietly to yourself, and meditating on the things of God ... those are the times when the Father notices.

As a Dad, I can tell you that the most important thing I want to cultivate in the lives of my children is this: that they know Jesus intimately. One day, I will be gone. They won't have their parents to talk to. But they will have Jesus Christ—which is our greatest gift to them. And Jesus is far more important. Jesus will minister to them for their entire lives.

One of the scariest passages in scripture is Matthew 7:21–23 when Jesus is describing Judgment Day.

> Not everyone who says to me, 'Lord, Lord,' will enter the kingdom of heaven, but only the one who does the will of my Father who is in heaven. Many will say to me on that day, 'Lord, Lord, did we not prophesy in your name and in your name drive out demons and in your name perform many miracles?' Then I will tell them plainly, 'I never knew you. Away from me, you evildoers!'

What that famous passage says to me is that God will not be fooled. We might fool the so-called "friends" and "followers" on our social media accounts, but we will not fool God. God sees right through all of that. In disgust, he will dismiss the hypocrites because they didn't even really know Him.

But those who know Jesus, who trust Him for their salvation, and who had a relationship—a true, meaningful, individual relationship with Him—those people will be welcomed by Jesus into the Kingdom of Heaven.

The message for us, is this: Save yourself from the corruption that this world offers. Do not allow yourself to make faith just a public affair. Make it your truth—in your intimate and private life.

And that means to spend time with God. Open up to Him every day. If you are sinning, then confess to Him, and ask him to help you with your struggles. Ask Him to lead you away from the temptations, just as the Lord taught us to pray in the Lord's Prayer. Talk to a friend who can serve as a mutual accountability partner. Have a confidential talk with a pastor, shepherd, deacon, or faithful Christian friend.

If you are worried about something, take it to the Lord in prayer. If you are angry, confess it to Christ so that you do not spew it onto your spouse. If you are lonely or sad, then go for a walk, and open up to Jesus, and tell him of your troubles. And then listen to what He says in return. Maybe he will answer you in your thoughts ... he might put something into your mind to help you.

Or he might send someone to talk with you. He might place his words into a sermon, so you feel like God is actually speaking to you. Many times, after I have preached, I have had people come up to me and say, "Pastor, that sermon was directed at me. There's no doubt in my mind that God spoke to me today through your sermon."

Or maybe you will pick up your Bible and you will read something that could only be a direct answer from God. Many people experience this phenomenon when they pick up their Bible and start reading.

According to the Bible, God communicates to us in many ways: dreams, scripture, sermons, friends, in the quiet of the night, or even in visions. The Bible has examples of all of these things happening. So be alert …. If you have an intimate relationship with Christ, you might be surprised to realize that God is actually communicating with you. He will answer your prayers. You are not alone. There is a God; He is alive. And he often communicates with His children.

In conclusion, following Jesus means—first and foremost—cultivating a relationship with Him. My prayer is that each of us will make faith a private thing first. And then if we choose to share our faith publicly, on social media, or whatever, then we will do that after we've developed intimate unity with the Lord in our hearts and minds.

My charge to you is that you seek God privately, whenever you get a chance. Maybe it is when you rise up in the morning. Maybe it is during your lunch break.

Maybe it is late at night when the day begins to quiet down. Maybe it is all throughout the day!

You will not regret this. You will feel refreshed. Developing an intimate relationship with God will work to your advantage as you experience greater closeness with your Heavenly Father. You will find yourself talking to Him throughout the day, and you will be enriched by the relationship you get to enjoy with your Creator.

2. We Are Not of this World

John chapter 17 is a very important passage of scripture known as the "High Priestly Prayer." Jesus is about to go to the cross, and he prays aloud to the Lord. During that powerful prayer, he says the following words to God, recounted in John 17:14–19:

> I have given them your word and the world has hated them, for they are not of the world any more than I am of the world. My prayer is not that you take them out of the world, but that you protect them from the evil one. They are not of the world, even as I am not of it. Sanctify them by the truth; your word is truth. As you sent me into the world, I have sent them into the world. For them I sanctify myself, that they too may be truly sanctified.

Those holy words will serve as our foundation for this chapter. In those verses, Jesus is saying that his followers, his disciples, the first Christians … they were hated in the world … and were persecuted and eventually killed. The world did not appreciate Jesus, and the world did not appreciate the disciples of Jesus. In many ways, this is still true because Christians often behave in ways that the world does not understand. And, as a result, the world often rejects us.

The second major idea that Jesus teaches here is that Christ doesn't want us to leave the world just yet. Rather, he wants God to protect us from Satan, just as Jesus prayed in the Lord's Prayer: "Lead us not into temptation, but deliver us from the evil one."

Then Jesus says, "They are not of this world, even as I am not of it." That is our focus for today, and it is a key idea. We are not of this world. We will look at that concept more carefully in a moment.

Then Jesus says, "Your word is truth." He's talking about the Holy Scriptures, God's word. That is where we have preserved God's word: in the Old and New Testaments. I am always a bit nervous when people stray away from the scriptures during Christian teaching. When preachers say things like, "I know the scriptures teach that, but it doesn't really mean that." As Christians, we must recognize what Jesus prayed here: "Lord, Your Word is Truth." If something conforms to God's Word, then it is true. If it does not, then as Christians, we at least keep it at arm's length. Or we outright reject it.

Finally, Jesus says to God that He has sent us into the world, which is a wonderful and comforting thought. Jesus says, "I have sent them into the world." If you combine this idea with verse 15—that Jesus does NOT want us to be taken out of the world—then you realize that God has put us into this world for a purpose.

Whenever you go through trials and challenges, the Lord Jesus does not want you to throw up your hands and give up. Jesus sent us into the world. We have been commissioned by Him. We are His partners on this earth. We should commit to staying on this earth until God calls us home. Sometimes it takes great perseverance, but like the apostle Paul, we realize that we have a great purpose. The apostle Paul tells us that sometimes he just wanted to leave the earth and be with the Lord. But listen to his conclusion in Philippians 1:22-24,

> If I am to go on living in the body, this will mean fruitful labor for me. Yet what shall I choose? I do not know! I am torn between the two: I desire to depart and be with Christ, which is better by far, but it is more necessary for you that I remain in the body.

Paul realized that other people needed him. And you and I need to realize that, too. You have people who will benefit from your life. There are people who need your encouragement, need your friendship, need your presence.

Jesus's high priestly prayer is commissioning us to do His will in the world. This is an important realization. You and I are missionaries. Jesus has so much work for us to do. He calls us to be salt and light. We are to intermix with people, both good and bad. Both Christians and non-Christians. We are to get involved with the messiness of life. We are to stay in here and keep working, keep meeting people, continue making an impact on behalf of our sender—Christ the Lord.

However, we are not of this world. What that means is this: "Our citizenship is in Heaven" (Philippians

3:20). In fact, that is a quotation from the apostle Paul in Philippians 3. We are not citizens of this earth. Our true citizenship is with God. Heaven is going to be our eternal home. And heaven is very different from the nations of the earth. Heaven is a monarchy. We have a benevolent king there, and Jesus reigns with him and sits at his right hand in the Royal Court.

What the New Testament teaches, however, is that the Kingdom of God is not just in heaven. It is on earth as well. We are citizens of that Kingdom, too. We are citizens of the Heavenly Nation, and God has given us a passport through our Baptism. So now we are on earth. We live here as aliens. Our true master is God, the king of Heaven. And Heaven is our true home. But for now, we're here.

We get to enjoy this life. It is wonderful to take walks with our spouse, go out to eat at delicious Italian restaurants, play softball with friends, or whatever. But we must always maintain our perspective. This world is not our true home. It is like a mid-priced motel. We sleep here for a few nights, with the basic necessities, but we're just passing through. We would never mistake our motel bed for our own bed. Similarly, our life is a journey right now.

So what am I saying? What is the point of all of this?

Here's the point: this earth can be wonderful one day, and brutal the next. The brutal days should be a reminder that we are missionaries here, not eternal citizens. And missionaries have to put up with a lot of opposition.

- We hear about wars going on … that's only on earth. Wars don't exist in Heaven.
- We read daily about violence, horrible accidents, and natural disasters. That's a terrible part of this world.
- We see people completely out of control on the internet, being hostile.
- We see division. People refusing to fellowship with each other.
- We see the homeless on the streets, broken both in spirit and in mind.
- We read about families breaking apart … divorces … mental anguish … broken people … children who have to choose which parent.

It can get depressing, sisters and brothers. But as Christians … as citizens of Heaven … we are to be missionaries to this suffering world. We are the ones who are supposed to be out there offering salve to a wounded and scarred population. We are Christ's body in a devastated world. We are His hands and feet.

Instead of getting on the internet and bullying a person, or putting them down, you and I are supposed to be the ones putting out fires. You and I are the ones who should be trying to reconcile people. You and I are supposed to be the ones calming the situation down, not pouring gasoline on the fire!

Recently, I read the results of a study. Here's what the person reporting on the study said: "If you want to be happy, stay off social media. A recent University of California study found that 'the more you use [social media] over time, the more likely you are to experience negative physical health, negative mental health and negative life satisfaction.'"

Why is that? They said these results apply even more towards young people who tend to compare themselves to what they are seeing, and they feel depressed after doing so. It fills them with negative emotions. And Facebook is pretty mild on these points, compared to Tik Tok, Instagram, and X.

Now, the Bible doesn't say to avoid social media. Rather, that's advice from science. I'm ambivalent about social media. It can be good for some people, but toxic for others. Some people love to connect with friends and send smiley faces ... which is wonderful. But the anger seething on social media today can be truly harmful for us if we're not careful.

Jesus is no respecter of persons. God shows no partiality. God stands so far above us. As Acts 10:34 says, "God accepts everyone who respects him and does what is right and acceptable to Him."

How should we be impacted from Jesus's words today that "we are not of this world?" It means that we should not put issues, or politics, or strongly held beliefs on the throne. Some people do this. When you talk to them, it's always about "those guys are doing this" ... we need to stick together and defeat the "bad guys" who are in the "bad guys" group.

That's the problem with getting overly committed to this place we call earth. For example, in a country that is about 50/50 ... you're going to get along swell with about 50 percent of the people, and you are going to be butting heads forever with that other 50 percent. This is not good for us as Christians! Jesus warns against selling our souls to the matters in this world. Our soul should remain with Him, and our highest loyalty should be to Him alone. We should be respectful, fair, and kind to all our brothers and sisters in Christ, whether they agree with our views or not.

Friends ... this world is our motel. It's not our home.

What if we were in North Korea right now? Those people are suffering. They have a dictator who won't relent. He kills people at his own whim. Their health care system is awful, and Christian doctors from South Korea are often brought in to treat them. Their citizens have no freedoms. They can't say anything against the government, or their "dear leader." In fact, they have to salute their leader as if they were saluting a god.

What if we were in Somalia right now, where the only way to make a good living is to get involved in crime? What if we lived in Colombia, where the most profitable and stable industry is drug-trafficking? What if we lived in Syria right now, where the national infrastructure is utterly decimated after the horrific reign of ISIS?

In all of those cases, this world is an awful place, and you have to struggle your whole life. It just doesn't seem fair that we get America, and they get a dictatorship, or a generational war, or a dollar a day.

Should we work hard to make America better for the have-nots! Yes, of course! By all means, we should all be doing that. We vote for the people we think will be best for our society. We pay taxes. We volunteer in the schools. We offer salve to a broken world … just like Jesus did. He offered hope and love. And we must do the same.

However … Jesus … he was not of this world. His commitment was to His Father.

And, oddly, when our true citizenship is in Heaven, we have a way of making this world a better place! (Did you catch that?) When you follow Jesus, you are good for this world. You are like salt to a meal. You are like light in the darkness. When you follow Jesus, and you refuse to get overly involved in the prejudices and arguments of this world … then somehow you end up being a blessing to the people around you.

America is an amazing place. Just live abroad for a while and you will see this clearly. But even still, I hope that we as a church can make this country—and our little corner in it—a better place.

We can't change the world. We can't change America. We can't change entire cities with all the millions of people in them.

But we can change a little, tiny part of our cities. We can bring light to the people in our circles. We can bring the hope of Jesus Christ to the people we interact with today. We can make our local church a shining lighthouse.

I'm reminded of the boy who was walking along the beach after a storm. He noticed thousands of starfish had washed ashore, and he was picking them up, one by one, throwing them back into the water.

A man walked up and said, "What are you doing, young man, you'll never save the lives of all those starfish. You might as well give up."

The boy picked up a starfish and looked at the man and said, "Well, I can save this one." He picked up another and said, "I can save this one."

Friends … let's get to work on behalf of our King … who is in Heaven. If we live our lives right—at this "motel" which is our temporary home—then He will welcome us into the Royal Palace on that special day, when he says to us, "Well done, thy good and faithful servant. Well-done."

I'll close with the scripture that we began with. Let's read it carefully one more time (John 17:14–19):

> I have given them your word and the world has hated them, for they are not of the world any more than I am of the world. My prayer is not that you take them out of the world but that you protect them from the evil one. They are not of the world, even as I am not of it. Sanctify them by the truth; your word is truth. As you sent me into the world, I have sent them into the world. For them I sanctify myself, that they too may be truly sanctified.

3. Choosing Your Team

We live in an individualistic society. We hear terms like a "self-made man" and "I'm looking out for #1." Our world often feels like eight billion individuals walking alone in a dangerous world, and only the strong will survive. Some people get really fired up, thinking it is them against the world. Some people even go through life alone … seemingly without a need for others. We call them "loners."

But trying to get through this life alone is a huge mistake. Ever since Genesis chapter 2, we learn that "It is not good for man to be alone." That's why God created Eve … so she could be a helpmeet to Adam. Together, they would face the world. And they created children. And you had the first family. From our very nature, from our biology, we are made to be with people.

We need people. We all remember COVID-19 in 2020-2021. We were forced to be alone much of the time. We were not with our normal teams. Unable to connect like we used to. Many of us had our wings clipped since we were unable to receive the fellowship, support, and physical contact that we needed. God created us to need people. And we were vehemently warned to "keep a safe distance." Remember the whole 6-feet thing? Or was it 10 feet? I forget.

One positive thing that took place during the depths of the pandemic was that I spent a lot of time with Sunde and our children. Indeed, that was a huge blessing. We watched a lot of movies, played together a whole lot on the beach, went on road trips, and I played a lot of Frisbee golf with Ross. If you ask my kids their favorite year they've ever had, I think they just might say, "during Covid!" We actually did have a lot of fun.

But one thing we definitely learned during that era—we need collaborators, we need companions, we need friends. We need Super Bowl parties. We need our colleagues at work. In business, we need people who will buy our products. Each of us are perpetually involved in daily transactions. Our bosses need us to pull our weight for our companies. There is constant give and take between ourselves and others.

Pretty much everybody is in this situation. It is a great blessing to buy and sell, to use and be used for good reasons, offer a hand up, and receive a hand out once in a while. We are involved in transactions each and every day. We need each other. We need people. The man was not created to be alone.

You need your manager down at your workplace. He needs you. You two will do much better if you learn how to dance well. Yes, you'll have problems with each other, but life is all about smoothing out problems, fixing them, and then moving on to new problems. That's life. A life without problems is called death!

You need that product on Amazon. So that means you also need the person in China who accepted your order over the internet, accepted your credit card, put your order in the system, and set the delivery of your product in order. You also need those tech-savvy people who activated your order in some big warehouse in Arizona. You need that man who drove your product from the Phoenix warehouse to the Los Angeles hub. Then, finally, you need that wonderful delivery man who picked up your product at 5:30am and dropped it at your house around supper time last night. You need all of them. They need your money, and you need what they have to offer you.

And this is life. I pay my doctor, and she keeps me and my family healthy. I pay Costco, and they keep my family fed. We pay our kids an allowance, and they do all sorts of helpful chores to keep our house clean and moving in an orderly fashion.

It has been said that there are two kinds of people in life: lifters and leaners. The truth is that we are both. There are times when we lift—I work hard nearly every day to provide my family with leadership and groceries and health insurance. But one of these days, the tables will turn, and I will need to lean on my wife and kids.

It is important for all of us to get this lesson figured out. You will never be recognized for your work, for your service, for your contributions … if you don't have people around you who recognize your work, your service, and your contributions. This is why we need organizations. We need teams. We need circles of friends. We need churches. We need companies. We need businesses that are connected to other businesses.

We are not alone. We are part of a flourishing society that needs reciprocity and cooperation to make things happen for all of us. And the quicker we figure this lesson out, the quicker we will get on the path to success.

This chapter deals with Jesus, and his need for a circle of people around him. Jesus was, obviously, a great leader. The greatest of all time. The most effective. But Jesus also had needs. He needed transactions. He needed help from His apostles—to spread the faith. And His apostles needed a life-purpose ... and they met each other's needs.

If we look in the gospels at Mark 1:17, we see Jesus went out and called his first disciples. The first one he called was Simon Peter, and Simon's brother Andrew. They were hardworking fishermen. Jesus made a proposition to them: "Come, follow me ... and I will make you fishers of men."

Next, Jesus called another set of brothers ... James and John. They, too, were fishermen there at the Sea of Galilee.

Then in Mark chapter 2, verse 14, we see Jesus calling a man named Levi. Now this one was surprising. Levi, also known as Matthew, was a tax collector. Tax collectors were despised in those days because they collected money from people, and they helped themselves to the money sometimes, and were known to be crooked. They profited in underhanded ways.

But Jesus gave this fellow a chance. Jesus saw something in Levi that nobody else saw. In fact, the people criticized Jesus for this choice, and Jesus said, "It is not the healthy who need a doctor, but the sick. I have not come to call the righteous, but sinners."

By the time we get to Mark chapter 3, verse 7, we see crowds of people following Jesus, and he has to choose his inner circle. And he chose 12 men. And this is where we get the expression, the "12 apostles." Out of all of his followers, Jesus chose his inner circle ... a group of 12 seemingly unimportant men: fishermen, tax collectors, a Zealot—political rebel—also named Simon, a very skeptical man named Thomas, a corrupt accountant by the name of Judas—who eventually betrayed Jesus and then felt so bad about it that he committed suicide.

But Jesus chose these 12 men. And you, too, must choose your inner circle. Remember, you are not alone. You need people who are close to you. You need an inner circle who can prop you up. So, you can lean on them. But you can also offer them something. Every relationship is transactional to some extent. You give and you receive. Any relationship that is only one-sided is probably distorted or unhealthy. Unless, of course, you are helping the vulnerable—like a baby or a sick or injured person. Like I said earlier, there are times in life when we lift, and there are times when we lean on others. Hopefully, we are doing both of those virtually all of the time.

Even Jesus was in a transactional relationship with his friends. He needed them to go out after his death and preach the gospel ... carrying the message to distant shores. He needed their loyalty. He needed their obedience. He needed them to carry on the great work of spreading the gospel. He needed them to be good examples of what the gospel can do to a person's life. He needed them to be courageous and willing to expand the kingdom of God on earth!

But they needed Jesus, too. They needed him desperately ... to give them purpose, to show them the way, and to understand the mission God had for them, and for everybody who gave their lives to Jesus.

Now, here's the lesson of this chapter ... you and I both need to select an inner circle. We need people around us to bolster us ... to lift us up ... to help us through the hard times. We need people to mourn with us. We need to people to celebrate our victories. We need an inner circle that functions on trust. It is a sacred thing to be chosen to be inside someone's inner circle.

Each of us needs to make a list of people we can really count on. I have a short list, just like you probably have. And it is important to think about it. You must be cognizant of it. Once you find a member of your inner circle, you need to fight for those relationships. You need to prove yourself to those people. You need to give to them, and allow them to give to you ... that's the glue of any relationship. There is give and take. You give your best to them, and you can count on them to give their best to you when you need them.

I am so thankful I have my wife, Sunde. She is my cornerstone. She is the most important person in my life. Together, we have thirty years of marriage!

We have four children. And I am giving them my best right now. Because one day I'm going to need them. I hope to God that my four children will fight for me whenever I need them. I hope and pray that my loyalty to them will come back to me in barrels. I give everything I have and everything I am to them right now ... and one day my hope is that they start helping Sunde and me along life's path, especially as we begin to slow down.

I am thankful to still have my mother. She is a rock to me. I can count on her. And she can count on me. We have an unbreakable bond. My father passed away on August 23, 2025. And, currently, my mother needs me, and I stand ready to help her. She is aging, and she needs her son to be ready to help her. I talk with my mother about 3–4 times a week because I value her. I treasure her. And I'm going to miss her when she goes to be with the Lord. Badly, I'll miss her. I know this from having just recently lost my Dad.

I have my church family. I have my shepherds and my ministry team! What a joy it is to work with them, and to call them friends. We have a very high level of trust.

Who is in your inner circle? Jesus chose 12 men. Of course, Jesus also had other people close to him. He had a very close relationship with his mother Mary. We are also told that he was extremely close to Mary, Martha, and Lazarus, the three siblings in Bethany that Jesus turned to time and again for support and restoration.

In conclusion, let me emphasize that you were created to be in groups. You are part of a nuclear family: mom, dad, and the kids. You are part of a religious family as well. You are part of several teams: at work, your friend-group, your neighborhood, and so forth. You are part of several meaningful groups, and your church family is one of the most important ones. A good church family will cause us all to be far healthier than if we had no church family.

So today, let us be reminded that we need people. Don't try to exist without an inner circle. You need people in your life ... people you can count on through thick and thin. Be devoted to them. Show them that you are going to stand up for them and their family. Fight for those relationships. Give to them. Receive from them. Enmesh your life with theirs. That's where the good stuff of life is. This is why it is so important that we offer Life Groups here at Hilltop. It's where depth takes place. We celebrate and mourn together, and pray together.

There will be hiccups along the way. Maybe you get a divorce. Those times are painful. Maybe someone in your inner circle betrays you ... like Judas Iscariot betrayed Jesus. But most of the time you can work those things out. Just like after Peter betrayed Jesus, our Lord figured out a way to restore Peter to the inner circle of friendship.

Friends, it is not good for you to be alone. You need others. So, show them respect and love. Don't take those relationships for granted. Don't let them slip away. Don't forget to pour into them.

May God bless our religious inner circles, that they might be places where trust is solid, where loyalty is firm, and where we always find ways to lift each other up, and to "lift up Jesus."

4. Live a Humble Life

Recently, I read an excellent book called *The Ideal Team Player* by Patrick Lencioni. It is not a Christian book. It is actually for businesspeople, and how to find the right people who will have the best chance at success in your company. I like to read self-improvement books, and this one made an impression on me.

The thesis of the book is that the best employees have three qualities: they are humble, hungry, and smart. That's it. This guy has sold hundreds of thousands of books telling people they need to be humble, hungry, and smart, and if they do those three things, then they will be successful.

Now, obviously, there is a lot to it. But I want to focus on that first one: humble. The author says humility is the most important of these three crucial traits.

He says people who are hungry are ambitious. And you want that in your company. You want people who strive to do their best. You also want smart people in your company. These are the types who make good decisions over and over. They figure things out. When faced with an obstacle, they figure out a way to get around it. They may not have several college degrees, but they are smart in the sense that they know how to get a job done. They know how to get along. They learn quickly.

Humility is the most important of the three traits, however. Humility, the author says, is ultimately more important than being hungry or smart. If you have humility, then you can improve. With humility, you realize it's not all about you. With humility, you can empathize with people. You have compassion. You're not a bulldozer. You realize that the people around you are as important as you are. When in an argument, you don't always demand your way because you have some humility about the situation.

The author says that without humility, ambitious people end up being bulldozers. They don't care ... they just want to win. They'll fire people without a second thought. People who lack humility often think the company revolves around themselves. They feel that they are "owed." Without humility, you become entitled ... or arrogantly perfectionistic. You walk around thinking people should just get out of your way because ultimately it is all about YOU and your desires.

This author says that people lack humility because they are, actually, insecure. This is counterintuitive. He says that people who have had a traumatic experience often feel like they aren't enough. They have been taught to feel they are worthless. Somebody hurt them and wounded them deeply. And the only way they know how to cope is to act big. They push others around. They over-achieve, and they'll knock you down to get what's theirs. Needless to say, they are not team players.

This book helped me a lot because it made me ask myself whether I am showing humility to the people around me. Sometimes I even make the mistake of thinking that my desires are what really matter, and I don't think enough about what others are facing. As long as my needs are met, then I'm good. But this is so wrong, on a number of levels.

The author suggests that if you struggle with insecurity and humility, then you should make yourself give compliments to others. Force yourself to say encouraging things to people when they succeed. Make it about them; not about you. After all, if you work in a team setting, the goal is for a team win, not just an individual score. You want the entire company to succeed. It's not about you. It's about the team.

Quarterback Tom Brady was famous for not asking for peak salary. He knew that if he was paid top salary, then his team would not be as good. The NFL operates by a "salary cap," which means each team has the same amount of money to spend. And if the quarterback eats it up, then you can't afford a good supporting cast. That's why Tom Brady went to 10 Super Bowls—he was paid less, which provided more money to recruit linemen who could protect Brady. My favorite team, the Dallas Cowboys, have the highest paid quarterback in the history of football ... and they haven't been to a Super Bowl in 30 years!

The *Ideal Team Player* book also emphasizes the importance of humility when it comes to admitting mistakes. You should admit mistakes when you make them. Swallow your pride. Don't get defensive. If someone points out a mistake you made, then say, "Yeah, you're right. I should work on that. Give me some tips that might help me in that regard."

In the history of Christianity, humility is the greatest of the virtues. Pride is considered the most dangerous sin because it can destroy you. And humility is considered the greatest strength because with humility you do all the things Jesus taught us to do:

- You put the needs of others ahead of your own.

- You serve others, rather than expecting them to serve you.

- You show that you are willing to improve, realizing you are not perfect.

- And you have a compassionate heart.

The Bible extolls the virtue of humility over and over. It should be no surprise that this concept is emphasized repeatedly in the Bible. Let's look at but a few of these passages:

- Colossians 3:12: Therefore, as God's chosen people, holy and dearly loved, clothe yourselves with compassion, kindness, humility, gentleness, and patience.

- Ephesians 4:2: Be completely humble and gentle; be patient, bearing with one another in love.

- James 4:6: God opposes the proud but shows favor to the humble.

- James 4:10: Humble yourselves before the Lord, and he will lift you up.

- 1 Peter 5:5: You who are younger, submit yourselves to your elders. All of you, clothe yourselves with humility toward one another because God opposes the proud but shows favor to the humble.

- Luke 14:11: All of those people who exalt themselves will be humbled, and those who humble themselves will be exalted.

Those are all wonderful passages. They hold the key to success in our professional, public, and Christian lives. With humility, we are closer to the heart of Christ. Jesus was completely humble. When we follow Jesus, we should have his same mindset.

I love that wonderful passage about humility in Philippians 2:5-8. Listen to this one:

> In your relationships with one another, have the
> same mindset as Christ Jesus: Who, being in very
> nature God, did not consider equality with God
> something to be used to his own advantage; rather,
> he made himself nothing by taking the very
> nature of a servant, being made in human
> likeness. And being found in appearance as a man,
> he humbled himself by becoming obedient to death
> —even death on a cross!

It's quite amazing that while Jesus was God's own son ... he was completely humble.

I once read an article in the *L.A. Times* about the son of a Persian Gulf nation's leader. He was a sheikh and his parents sent him to USC (University of Southern California) to attend college. All those years, he stayed in the same hotel that Julia Roberts was in the movie "Pretty Woman." He walked around with an entourage. He hardly ever attended classes, and instead, he hired a graduate student to do all of his work via Zoom, citing "security concerns" for why he couldn't actually attend class. He had the finest cars, equipped with drivers.

Yet Jesus was God's own son! And he chose to live with humility. He recruited simple fishermen as his close circle of friends. He gave attention to people living on the margins of society. When people attacked him, he prayed that God might forgive them. When people experienced shame and disgrace, Jesus lifted them up and ministered to them.

We serve a powerful God. But we also have a Lord who knows what humility is.

As you all know, I love the book of Proverbs. Listen to some of these great passages about humility in the Proverbs:

- 11:2: When pride comes, then comes disgrace, but with humility comes wisdom.

- 27:2: Let someone else praise you, and not your own mouth; an outsider, and not your own lips.

- 18:2: Before a downfall the heart is haughty, but humility comes before honor.

So, what am I saying in this chapter? I am saying that we all need to have an aura of humility about us. It will keep us out of trouble. It will show others that we are not just all about ourselves, but we are all about them as well. And it will show that we are trying to follow Jesus in how we conduct ourselves with other people.

A few years ago, on Facebook, one of my old high school friends wrote, "Dyron, what do you make of all of this chaos going on in our society right now," or something like that. It was right at the height of all of those social eruptions we were having. We were all wearing masks and watching scary nightly reports on the news. It was a frustrating era.

I can tell you what would have happened had I spouted off my opinions about everything under the sun, from politics to pandemics ... I would have had about 16 online quarrels that day. And I don't have time for that nonsense. None of us do. It's a complete waste of time to participate in those insulting arguments online, that resolve absolutely nothing.

So, in return, I wrote one of the most important passages in all the Bible. It is found in Micah 6:8: "What does the Lord require of you? To act justly and to love mercy and to walk humbly with your God."

I believe strongly that humility is the solution to so many of the problems we are having in our society these days. We need to be humble in public. Humble online. We should humble ourselves in the presence of others that God may lift us up, rather than acting as if we are quite important.

Our society is so full of pride right now, sisters and brothers. We have people who are just longing for a fight. They want to argue on social media, so they can push others down. People will call each other out on some little thing. When you pull into a parking spot, people will give you the meanest look, just because you happened to park in a spot that they don't approve of.

Some people act like arrogant wolves. They're just looking for someone to pounce on.

But you, be humble. Have the spirit of God in you. Allow the Holy Spirit into your heart and mind so that you can say "no" to that egotism. Allow Christ to touch your heart so that you have compassion on people. Show kindness, to the arrogant as well as to the broken. Show servanthood. As Jesus says, if someone asks you to go one mile with them, then go two.

The world needs some humility right now, brothers and sisters. Ask God to make you more humble. You are on the right track if you humble yourself before God, and prioritize the needs of others ahead of your own.

5. How to Deal with the Ahabs and Jezebels

Have you ever been subjected to mistreatment by another person?

This mistreatment can come in a variety of ways.

- Perhaps someone cheated you in a business deal;
- Perhaps someone took advantage of you;
- Perhaps someone slandered you, falsely accused you, or spoke maliciously against you;
- Perhaps someone you thought was a friend totally turned on you.

I think we can all relate to these painful things. Some of you may have been mistreated by a co-worker. Or even a family member! (That one hurts really bad!) Some have been hurt by strangers who were up to no good. Some of you may have been mistreated by a spouse or someone you loved deeply. Many of us have been mistreated by a superior, by a boss, or by a person in power who held the keys to our future.

Unfortunately, I think all of us have been subjected to one or more of these things. And the most common reaction is to give them a taste of their own medicine. Get them right back. Flesh for flesh. Eye for eye, tooth for tooth. These are the times we naturally want to go to the Old Testament, when we should actually try to go more to the New Testament teachings of Jesus.

Unfortunately, many of us deal with mistreatment by doling out mistreatment. That is the natural course of things. We feel like they wronged us, so it is our turn to wrong them.

But you know what? There is nothing Christian about this approach to mistreatment.

The stories of the Bible feature many people who behaved badly. Almost every book in the Bible has examples. And, in reality, those kinds of people are always among us. As Jesus says, the devil is out to steal, kill, and destroy. And some people decide to go that way in life, rather than in the direction of Jesus.

Usually, these folks are hurting deep inside of themselves. And as we all know, "Hurt people hurt people." And I suspect many of us have been hurt by these hurt people. These people can really wound us. And, unfortunately, these people often bring out the worst in us. In some cases, if we are not careful, they can distort us, and we become something we didn't want to become.

It is common to hear stories about predators, bullies, and evildoers. When they get arrested, we find out that they themselves were taken advantage of when they were children. Something went wrong in their childhood, and it has stayed with them. And they allowed those experiences to ruin their sense of compassion and goodness.

Following Jesus

I am reminded of the woman Jezebel in the Bible. Boy, she was rough. Not many people go around naming their daughters Jezebel these days, and for good reason.

Jezebel is one of the main characters in the Old Testament book of 1 Kings. She was actually the wife of one of the Jewish kings, a man named Ahab. Ahab was one of the wicked kings of Israel. But his wife Jezebel was probably worse than him.

Just listen to Jezebel's rap sheet:

- She tried to get the Israelites to stop worshiping God, and instead she instituted the worship of a god named Ba'al. She also instituted the Asherah religion—which required the sordid practice of temple prostitution.

- Jezebel had statues built honoring other gods, and she put them all around the Jewish people so they would start worshiping these other gods.

- She hired hundreds of priests and prophets to practice these other religions in order to get the people to abandon the worship of Yahweh/Jehovah—the God of Abraham, Isaac, Jacob, and of course, the God we worship today in Christianity.

- She systematically purged the Jewish religion by pulling down any altars that were for the worship of Yahweh.

- She had the prophets and priests of Israel assassinated, one by one, until only 100 were left who maintained loyalty to Yahweh. It got to the point that the Israelite people were split between worshiping God or worshiping the fertility cults that Jezebel introduced.

- There is one famous story about Jezebel that just makes the blood boil. Jezebel's husband, King Ahab, wanted to expand his property. So Ahab went down to the owner of the adjacent property to ask him how much it would take to buy him out. The man—named Naboth—said his vineyard was too important for him. It was his family's land, and he didn't want to give it up for any amount of money. It was far too important to him to sell, even to the king. Naboth inherited it from his ancestors, and he would pass it on to his children and to their children.

- So, King Ahab got really defeated and depressed and sullen and walked back to his palace. They say he quit eating, he was so depressed about it. His wife, Jezebel, asked him what was wrong. He told her, "I went down to talk to the owner of the adjacent property—a man named Naboth—and he would not sell me his property. So now I cannot take over his property and expand my vineyards into that direction."

- Well, Jezebel was not about to take "no" as an answer from a commoner like Naboth. She asked her husband, *"Are you not the king?"* So she then orchestrated a plan. She hired some false witnesses to say they witnessed Naboth cursing God and cursing her husband Ahab the king. And since he cursed the king, he was required by law to be stoned to death. So they dragged this innocent man outside the city gates and stoned him to death. The Bible tells us the morbid detail that dogs came to Naboth's corpse and licked his blood. (This little bit becomes important later on.) His sons were put to death, too (2 Kings 9:26), so they could not inherit the land.

- King Ahab was happy now. Not only was Naboth dead, but now King Ahab was able to go and get the property. After all, Naboth was now under condemnation by everyone, including the government. His name was ruined, all because of Jezebel's lies. The Bible says Ahab then "Got up and went to take over the vineyard."

- But God came into the scene at this point. And God said in 1 Kings 21:19, "Ahab, you murdered Naboth and took his property. And so, in the very spot where dogs licked Naboth's blood, they will lick up your blood." God also said Jezebel would meet a similar fate, and would have her corpse completely devoured by dogs.

- God also promised to rip the monarchy out of the hands of both Ahab and his wife Jezebel, and pass on the power of the kingdom to a warrior named Jehu. Jehu indeed took over the kingship and reigned for 28 years, and his children inherited the throne after him.

- Jezebel and Ahab not only lost their lives, but they lost the kingdom, as God took it out of their hands and gave it to another family.

Here's how the end of this long story is described in the Bible, in 2 Kings 9:30-37:

> Jehu headed toward Jezreel, and when Jezebel heard he was coming, she put on eye shadow and brushed her hair. Then she stood at the window, waiting for him to arrive. As he walked through the city gate, she shouted down to him, "Why did you come here, you murderer? To kill the king? You're no better than Zimri!"
>
> He looked up toward the window and asked, "Is anyone up there on my side?" A few palace workers stuck their heads out of a window, and Jehu shouted, "Throw her out the window!" They threw her down, and her blood splattered on the walls and on the horses that trampled her body.
>
> Jehu left to get something to eat and drink. Then he told some workers, "Even though she was evil, she was a king's daughter, so make sure she has a proper burial."
>
> But when they went out to bury her body, they found only her skull, her hands, and her feet. They reported this to Jehu, and he said, "The Lord told Elijah the prophet that Jezebel's body would be eaten by dogs right here in Jezreel. And he warned that her bones would be spread all over the ground like manure, so that no one could tell who it was."

Most of us have had a Jezebel or an Ahab in our lives. Have you ever had a person who mistreated you pretty badly? Have you had a person who lied about you, or even to you?

Well, in a strange way, I have good news for you. You can let it go. That's right, you can move on. Why? Because God is a just God, and He will take care of you. If you trust Him, He will take care of the Jezebels and the Ahabs in your life. God will restore you, and He will protect you and your family.

Even Naboth ... he was killed, but God took care of his family. God restored his name, and here we are, nearly 3000 years later, talking about the integrity of Naboth, as opposed to the viciousness of Ahab and Jezebel.

Yes, God will protect you from the Jezebels. And not only will God protect you, but those people who harmed you will have to face God eventually. And the justice of God is a concept that is clear in the Bible.

However, it is important that we should not take vengeance ourselves. As followers of Christ, we allow God to take care of the situation. And He will.

Just like in the case of Jezebel ... her craftiness and cruelty did not pay off. Rather, it backfired. And not only was she disposed of in a horrible way, but her entire family was cut off.

Both in the Old and New Testaments, God promises that He will take vengeance against the wrongdoer. In Deuteronomy 32:35, we read this:

> It is mine to avenge; I will repay.
> In due time, their foot will slip;
> their day of disaster is near
> and their doom rushes upon them.

Similarly, in Romans 12:19, Paul quotes that verse, and writes:

> Do not take revenge, my dear friends, but leave room for God's wrath, for it is written: "It is mine to avenge; I will repay," says the Lord.

Jesus said the following in Matthew 5:

> You have heard that it was said, 'Love your neighbor and hate your enemy.' But I tell you, love your enemies and pray for those who persecute you, that you may be children of your Father in heaven. He causes his sun to rise on the evil and the good, and sends rain on the righteous and the unrighteous. If you love those who love you, what reward will you get? Are not even the tax collectors doing that? And if you greet only your own people, what are you doing more than others? Do not even pagans do that? Be perfect, therefore, as your heavenly Father is perfect.

In conclusion, let us remember that "getting back" at people is never our approach, as Christians. Our goal is to do the best we can, treat people well, and live our lives with humility—like we talked about last week. And when we are mistreated, we are to leave it up to God ... and allow God to work it all out in the end because He will. And you don't want to get involved with that. When God takes vengeance upon people, He goes all out. That is God's justice. He can do that because He makes the rules.

And if you have bitterness in your heart towards that person who maligned you, spoke ill of you, or hurt you deeply ... trust that God will work all of that out of you in time. You will only hurt yourself by seeking to avenge yourself.

Friends, as Christians, this lesson should be very comforting. People may come at you in this life. But you can deflect them. And just do your best to forgive them — although I realize forgiving is extremely hard to do. Probably the hardest thing to do that there is as humans.

And let us not gloat when we see our enemies fall or come to ruin by God's mighty hand. Like Jesus said, and as He did … our job is to forgive them. Our duty is to live by the principle of love. God will handle the equalizing. God will dole out the justice. He promised us this in Hebrews 10:

> For we know him who said, "It is mine to avenge; I will repay," and again, "The Lord will judge his people." It is a dreadful thing to fall into the hands of the living God.

Let us allow room for God's wrath. We make a big mistake if we try to take that upon ourselves.

One time I was hurt by someone, and a friend of mine gave me great advice … he said, "Whatever you do, don't become like them."

Let us keep on "Following Jesus." Follow Him to the best of your ability, and stay focused exactly on him.

And remember to leave the Jezebels and the Ahabs alone. God will take care of them.

6. God's Providential Protection

This chapter is about how blessed we are as Christians because God almighty protects us from harm, from ruin, and from hopelessness whenever we put ourselves underneath His protection.

A couple of years ago, my parents had an experience that seemed like a story right out of the Bible. It was the 4th of July, and they decided to go to bed. Their neighbors stayed up lighting fireworks and hanging out while sitting on their front porch. Their neighbor is named Floyd, and he is actually one of my childhood friends. We grew up together and graduated the same year.

Well, at some point late in the evening, my dad was already fast asleep. He has a health issue, so he takes medicine to help him sleep, and he was utterly wiped out. My mom was in bed, too, about to put her earplugs in, as she wears them to prevent her from waking up, since she is a light sleeper.

I'm from New Mexico. It is a very dry part of the world. It had not rained in months, and was completely bone-dry outside. And that doesn't mix well with fireworks. And, wouldn't you know it … fireworks caught the field on fire right behind my parents' house. The field was burning as fast as an old, dry barn when the fire started racing towards their house. Problem was, my parents were completely unaware of it since they were fast asleep, with earplugs in.

That's when my mom heard a strange banging on the door, and the ringing of the doorbell. So she went to the door, and there was my friend Floyd. He is an EMT and a firefighter. He knew they only had a few minutes before my parents' house would go up in flames. He told them they had no time to waste, and they must immediately get themselves out of the house and into the street.

My mother rushed to my dad's room to wake him up, but he was in a deep sleep. Then, suddenly, there was a huge "BANG" in the air that sounded like a bomb had gone off. My mother wondered if the fire had exploded a gas tank or something, since it was so terribly loud.

Then all of a sudden, rain started absolutely pouring down … like cats and dogs. It was a rain unlike anything they had seen in years. And it was pouring and pouring with huge thunderbolts and lightning. The sudden rainstorm had knocked down the fire, and as suddenly as the fire rose, there was no longer any danger. The heavens just opened up and put the fire out. That fire was no match for that massive downpour that night.

Now, that's what I call God's providential protection. My parents serve the Lord. And when a fire came screaming at their home, God provided a miracle. For God, a massive fire is nothing. God can just send a rainstorm out of nowhere. It hadn't rained in 3 months.

It was dangerously dry! Why did it happen to rain just right then and there? No rain was even in the forecast. It just poured and poured. The fire was suddenly out. Nobody was hurt, everyone and everything was safe.

But had that fire not been put out by rain, then God would have used a fireman to save my parents. My childhood friend Floyd would have come to their rescue had that rainstorm not suddenly arrived. In fact, Floyd was already there!

Friends, not only will God protect you, but He will also provide a backup plan just in case. God protects us.

I am reminded of Exodus 14:14, *The LORD will fight for you; you need only to be still.*

You may have heard of the story of God's prophet Elisha in 2 Kings 6. Elisha was God's foremost prophet on the earth at that time. The king of Aram (modern-day Syria) decided to send an army to capture Elisha and kill him so he wouldn't be able to help the Israelites win the war. The army followed Elisha and his servant. Eventually, they caught up to them and surrounded them. Elisha's servant became fearful because they were sure to die at this moment.

But then Elisha prayed to God, "Lord, please open the eyes of my servant so that he may see" (2 Kings 6:17). Right then and there, God opened the eyes of Elisha's servant, and he saw a vast army of angels, with chariots and horses; they had surrounded the army of Aram.

The Bible makes it clear ... that army of angels was there, whether anyone else could see them or not. God provides angels for our protection, and usually, we don't even see them. Although the Bible teaches that sometimes we see angels, we just aren't aware that they are angels. They are sent by God. We just didn't recognize it at the time. Hebrews says, "Do not forget to show hospitality to strangers, for by so doing some people have shown hospitality to angels without knowing it" (Hebrews 13:2).

Back to our story ... then Elisha asked God to strike the army of Aram with blindness, and they became temporarily blind. They were utterly powerless now that they were blind. So, Elisha led them to the Israelites, and the Israelite king was actually going to put them to death.

But it is amazing what Elisha did ... he said, "No, do not kill them. Rather, set food and water before them so that they may eat and drink and then go back to their master" (2 Kings 6:22)

Then, we are told that Elisha had a great feast prepared for their enemies, the army of Aram. And then the text says, "So the bands from Aram stopped raiding Israel's territory, because of this kindness expressed to them." (2 Kings 6:23)

Elisha actually prepared a table for them in the presence of his enemies, just as the 23rd Psalm talks about (Psalm 23:5).

It was a stroke of genius for Elisha. The king of Aram decided to stop invading Israel, and the two nations actually became allies. Elisha was so courageous. He knew God would deliver him. And not only would God save him and his servant with an angelic army, but God also provided a backup plan: striking that army with blindness.

But if that wasn't enough, Elisha, the man of God, decided to have mercy upon the army of Aram. He forgave them, and even had a banquet prepared for them.

That story shows the power of God's providential protection.

Perhaps sometimes we doubt the Lord. We doubt whether he can help us in a given situation. But doubt is the reason our prayers are not answered most of the time.

Listen to the words of James 1:6-8:

> When you ask, you must believe and not doubt because the one who doubts is like a wave of the sea, blown and tossed by the wind. That person should not expect to receive anything from the Lord. Such a person is double-minded and unstable in all they do.

You see, friends, God appreciates it when we ask him to help us. But we can't just ask. We have to expect. We must expect God to answer our prayers. We must believe that God is real, that he is all-powerful. That he is able to help us.

When we doubt God, it is like we are showing that we don't really have faith in what he can do. It is like we are "double-minded." We ask him, but we do not expect him to do anything. This should not be.

So let me conclude this chapter by encouraging us all to "trust" in God's providential protection. Has God saved you from any fires or other emergencies? Has

God caused you to go this way, when had you gone the other way it would have been a disaster?

I place my trust in God because I know that God will protect me. I will trust in God when it looks like I am surrounded by enemies. I will hope in the Lord when it looks like I am outnumbered.

We must trust in God's providential protection, but we must believe and not doubt. We must trust God for our very life and breath.

God has decreed in His word, in Hebrews 9:27, "It is appointed unto men once to die, but after this the judgment."

So, of course, we'll eventually die. God has an appointed time for you. But that's no big deal for God. There again, even when faced with death, you have to trust in God's providential protection. You have to know in your heart that you will be saved. Romans 10:9 says, "If you declare with your mouth, 'Jesus is Lord,' and believe in your heart that God raised him from the dead, then you will be saved."

Any difficult trial, any storm, any fire, any enemy is nothing compared to the power of God. God can send a huge thunderstorm to put out your fires. God can save you from danger. God can extend your life. God can even save your soul from hell. Jesus says,

> Do not be afraid of those who kill the body but cannot kill the soul. Rather, fear the one who can destroy both soul and body in hell. (Matthew 10:28).

And, if you trust him, He will save you. He will see you through ... if you believe it in your heart. If you fear God. If you commit to God through the waters of baptism.

If you trust in Christ like this, then not even death should intimidate you. You are providentially protected.

And that is precisely why Jesus had such courage. He knew that even death was but nothing to God. It was a mere "crossing over." God's word says, "Each of us are appointed to die once, and after that to face the judgment (Hebrews 9:27)." Each one of us has an appointed time when we shall stop breathing. God has promised this. But everlasting life awaits if we trust in Him to walk us through the valley of the shadow of death.

Remember ... there are always things going on in the world that can cause us to fear if we let it. Potential financial collapse. Illness, plague, health scares. There are other misfortunes that can happen.

But let us *fear not*. For God is with us. None of these things are of any power when compared to God. Whom shall we fear? Nobody. There is no reason to fear anybody, any disaster, any illness, any loss of income. God will take care of you.

God will send his army of angels. He will send rain. He will send a new job to you. He will send you money when you least expected it. He will send you a wonderful person just when you thought you were destined to be alone. He will send you opportunities, and joy, and love. God will send you a lifeline. Jeremiah 29:11 says, "For I know the plans I have for you," declares the

LORD, "plans to prosper you and not to harm you, plans to give you hope and a future."

I will end this chapter with the final words of Jesus when he was on this earth. He had just resurrected, and he was about to ascend back to the Father. And here is what he said (Matt. 28:18-20):

> All authority in heaven and on earth has been given to me. Therefore, go and make disciples of all nations, baptizing them in the name of the Father and of the Son and of the Holy Spirit, and teaching them to obey everything I have commanded you. And surely I am with you always, to the very end of the age.

Amen, Jesus. We know you are with us.

7. The Power of Perception

I once heard about a young man from California who was thinking about possibly moving to Boston. There was a job opening there that he was interested in. The company flew him out to interview, and he passed the interview with flying colors, and they offered him the job on the spot.

The only problem, however, was that he wasn't sure that he wanted to move to the East Coast. He had never visited there. He had no family on the East Coast. It was a completely different culture for him. All he knew was California.

So, he was walking along the Massachusetts shore line that same evening that he received the job offer, and he was considering what to do. As he was walking along, enjoying the sunset, he encountered a couple. They, too, were walking along the beach, enjoying the evening. So he struck up a conversation. He told them he was thinking about moving there, and he asked them what the people were like in Boston. Are they friendly? Are they kind? What are they like?

The couple snarled their noses and said, "This is a cut-throat culture. People are selfish here. They will cut you down just to get ahead. Here on the East Coast, people are stuck up and rarely talk to you. It is very difficult to get plugged in here. You'll find it hard to make any friendships in Boston."

The young man thanked them, and then went back to walking on the beach. He said to himself, "Whew, I dodged a bullet. I'm going to turn down that job offer because I could never work in a place like this. I'm better off staying put in California. Why would I want to move to Boston, where everybody acts like that?"

The young man started walking again, and after a little while he encountered another couple. He thought to himself, "Well, I should probably ask them what they think about the East Coast, just to see what they say."

So he struck up a conversation with this new couple. He told them about his job offer, and he asked them what people were like in Boston, and on the East Coast in general.

The couple responded, "People here are amazing. They are kind and caring. They are very friendly if you try to get to know them. Once you make a friend here on the East Coast, you have a friend for life. Here in Boston, people will step up for you; they'll treat you like family."

The young man thanked them, and kept walking along. He scratched his head because now he was perplexed. The first couple acted like the East Coast was the worst place to live in America. The second couple gave the opposite response, making him want to move to Boston as soon as he possibly could. It sounded like a great place to start a family and put down some roots.

So, the young man kept walking. Eventually, he encountered an elderly gentleman walking along. He thought to himself, "Why not try one more time ... just to see what happens." A bit of a tie-breaker. So he spoke to the elderly man, "Sir, I am thinking about moving here to Boston. But I'm unsure because I don't know what the people are like here. I got a good job offer, but I don't want to move here, only to end up regretting it. So, sir, can you please tell me what the people are like here?"

The wise old gentleman said, "Well, first, let me ask you a question. What are the people like in California?"

The young man looked down at the sand and thought about it for a moment. Then he looked back up at the old man and said, "People in California are wonderful. They tend to be very kind and caring. I have some wonderful friends in California, people who love me for me."

The elderly gentleman then said, "Well, then that's exactly how you'll find the people on the East Coast. It's not about the people. It's about your perception of them." The elderly gentleman then smiled, shook the young man's hand, and walked away into the sunset.

The young man then realized what the elderly gentleman said was absolutely true. "It's not about the people. It's about your perception of them."

Sisters and brothers, people are people. You're going to find awesome people all over God's beautiful creation. You're going to find some bad apples in every town, city, and village, too. But your perception is what will make all the difference.

If you view people as basically good and kind and trustworthy. Then guess what? They will be basically good and kind and trustworthy. If you are suspicious of people, thinking they should not be trusted. Then guess what? Your views will probably be fairly accurate. It's all about your perception.

Let's read a passage from the Gospel of Mark. It is located at Mark 2:13–17:

> Once again, Jesus went out beside the lake. A large crowd came to him, and he began to teach them. As he walked along, he saw Levi, son of Alphaeus, sitting at the tax collector's booth. "Follow me," Jesus told him, and Levi got up and followed him.
>
> While Jesus was having dinner at Levi's house, many tax collectors and sinners were eating with him and his disciples, for there were many who followed him. When the teachers of the law who were Pharisees saw him eating with the sinners and tax collectors, they asked his disciples: "Why does he eat with tax collectors and sinners?"
>
> On hearing this, Jesus said to them, "It is not the healthy who need a doctor, but the sick. I have not come to call the righteous, but sinners."

What this passage of scripture teaches us is the power of perception. Jesus chose to see these "sinners" as people worthy of his time and energy. Jesus wanted to help them. "It's not the healthy who need a doctor, but the sick," he said.

Jesus saw possibilities with these people. Jesus chose to think positive thoughts about their potential. Instead of being suspicious of these "sinners"—these wealthy, upper-class people—Jesus saw them as potential friends.

And the interesting thing here is that Jesus made disciples out of these people. Jesus invested in them, so they invested in him.

You see, your perception is everything. If you view your spouse in a negative, pessimistic way, then guess what your spouse will be like? But if you view your spouse with tenderness and compassion and understanding, then guess what your spouse will probably be like?

It's the same with your family. Same with your co-workers. Same with your peers and colleagues. Same with people on the street. If your outlook is one of suspicion and pessimism, then guess what your world will look like!

You may know the story of the famous psychiatrist Viktor Frankl. He was a Jew who ended up in Hitler's concentration camps during World War Two. While in unspeakably horrific conditions, he came to realize the power of his perception.

The pessimists around him deteriorated and became selfish, and eventually gave up hope and died. But Frankl, and a few others, held on to hope. They chose to imagine the world as a humane place for the most part. He came to realize that the Nazis were only a fraction of humanity, and they didn't represent all humans. Plus, he came to realize that the camps were much more tolerable if he chose to view people as potential friends, in need of camaraderie and fellowship.

So, Frankl built friendships with people, even in the camps. He treated people humanely, and focused on what his world could be if a few people were good and kind and friendly to each other. And it not only helped him to have a better attitude, it actually kept him alive.

I am reminded of Nelson Mandela, the great South African leader who was in prison from 1962 to 1990 because he questioned the nation's policy of racial segregation. He was a person of dignity within the prison in South Africa, where blacks and whites were separated according to the laws of apartheid. He always maintained his self-assurance and poise. He encouraged other prisoners. He was revered by all the prisoners, and even many of the guards. He shadow-boxed and pretended he was jumping rope in order to stay in shape. He did all this for 27 years, and was then released, and shortly thereafter became president of South Africa.

Mandela held on to his dignity. He knew that he was above his circumstances. He never allowed his perception to sour or to become overwhelmed with negativity. He kept his chin up and survived. Not only did he survive, but he came out on top, and was able to oversee the end of apartheid and a new era of racial integration in South Africa. He refused to turn against his fellow countrymen. He refused to participate in "payback." He treated his oppressors with dignity. He realized that someone must stop the hate, the suspicion, and the violence. And he gave his life to being that person.

Sisters and brothers ... perception is huge. If you choose to see hope in the world ... then there will be hope. If you choose to see the possibility of change in your spouse, then you just might save your marriage. If you are able to change your perception about that colleague that you have grown to hate, then maybe, just maybe, you can turn that person into a good friend with time. You just have to change your perception of them. Your goodness toward them may help them to see you in a more positive light, too.

I want to close with a story about a football game in the city of Grapevine, Texas, in 2008. It was one of the strangest games in football history.

Grapevine Christian High School was hosting the Gainesville State School, which is actually in the town where my wife is from. In fact, she grew up just down the road from the State School, which is not really a school. It is a prison for high school kids. Kids who were never wanted. Kids who committed crimes. Kids who had been cast out of society, into a youth prison.

With good behavior, the boys at the Gainesville State School could play on the football team and travel for games. They had no home stadium. Prisons don't have home stadiums. Every single one of their games is "on the road." This helps to explain why they never win games. They only lose their games. And this particular season, they were 0-9. Zero wins, nine losses. As usual.

Well, on this particular Friday night, the State School kids went to play Grapevine Christian High, a school in the Dallas area. However, something was very odd when the young prisoners ran out of the locker room onto the field that night. There was one of those big paper banners for them to run through. People were cheering. They looked up into the stands and saw 50% of the crowd on their side, and 50% of the crowd on the other side. Normally, their side of the stands were completely empty. They had never had their own fans because they had never played at home.

But the Grapevine Christian fans had planned in advance that they would split up their own fans. Half of their fans would act as if the young prisoners were their own boys. And they cheered the State School kids with all their might for four quarters.

Now, Grapevine Christian High School had a powerhouse football team every year. And Grapevine actually won the game without any trouble. However, the State School kids felt as if they had won the state title! They were all smiling and slapping high-fives. They had hundreds of people cheering them on for four quarters, and it felt so wonderful. People had actually cheered for them!

After the game, the coaches met at mid-field to pray with all the players. They asked one of the State School boys to lead the prayer. The young man bowed his head and with a strong voice prayed, "Lord I don't know how this happened, so I don't know how to say thank You, but I never would've known there were so many people in the world that cared about us."

After the game, the Grapevine Christian kids walked the State School boys to the bus, and handed them each a bag – with a burger, fries, soda, candy, a Bible, and an encouraging letter from one of the Grapevine Christian players.

As the bus drove off, the young team from the State School in Gainesville headed back to their penitentiary, but they all had their hands and noses on the windows, looking with amazement at these people who cheered for them, accepted them as equals, treated them with respect, and prayed with them. They were absolutely shocked by the love they experienced that evening in the city of Grapevine. For but a few hours, they were not prisoners, they were high school football players.

Everything is about perception. You can change people with a healthy outlook. You can change yourself through the power of perception. You can be like Jesus if you choose to see the people around you with hope, with trust, and with kindness. You can change the world with the power of perception.

> When the teachers of the law who were Pharisees saw him eating with the sinners and tax collectors, they asked his disciples: "Why does he eat with tax collectors and sinners?"
>
> On hearing this, Jesus said to them, "It is not the healthy who need a doctor, but the sick. I have not come to call the righteous, but sinners." (Mark 2:16–17)

When you and I see "sinners," we often look down on them, or we view them with suspicion. However, Jesus sees them as potential disciples.

So, when we try to move to a place of "following Jesus," then we, too, should try to view "sinners" with compassion. Like Jesus, instead of viewing people as simply "enemies," then maybe we should see them as potential disciples of the Lord Jesus Christ.

After all, you and I are sinners, too. I am thankful to God that he didn't just turn His back on me. God's perception of me gave me hope. And God's perception of me changed me. And God's perception of you probably changed you, too.

And maybe, just maybe, your perception of someone could change as well. Perhaps your perception of them will give them hope. And maybe God will use all of that to bring them to Himself.

Following Jesus means that we refuse to "dismiss" people. Rather, we see them as potential brothers and sisters in Christ.

8. The Tale of Two Chameleons

There's a saying that goes like this: "You've got to take a stand for something, or you'll fall for anything." This is actually the title of a country music hit in the early 1990s. And I believe it is absolutely true.

Have you ever known someone who is wishy-washy? They will say one thing to your face, and then they'll say something else behind your back? We often describe these kinds of people as lacking a backbone.

They're chameleons. You know what chameleons are famous for. They are fascinating little lizards with a curly tail at the very end. They are native to very warm climates in Africa, tropical Asia, and Southern Europe. They are often adopted as household pets. But what they are most famous for is being able to fit in to their surroundings. Their skin color changes based on what kind of conditions they are in. If you see a chameleon on a branch, it will turn brown. If you see it on or near leaves, it will turn leafy green. When it starts to get dark, chameleons will often turn black. They are amazing creatures for this reason, and that's why we have brought them into the English vocabulary.

However, being a chameleon is an important thing to do sometimes. What do I mean by this? Well, the apostle Paul, in 1 Corinthians 9, says this ...

> Though I am free and belong to no one, I have made myself a slave to everyone, to win as many as possible. To the Jews I became like a Jew, to win the Jews. To those under the law, I became like one under the law (though I myself am not under the law), so as to win those under the law. To those not having the law, I became like one not having the law (though I am not free from God's law but am under Christ's law), so as to win those not having the law. To the weak I became weak, to win the weak. I have become all things to all people so that by all possible means I might save some. I do all this for the sake of the gospel, that I may share in its blessings.

What Paul is telling us here is that you need to be a chameleon sometimes. You need to be able to adapt to your surroundings in order to "win as many as possible."

Our job, as Christians, is "to win as many as possible." This is one of the biggest failings of the American church today. We fuss and fight about politics, we scream at each other on social media, we condemn people with whom we disagree. But we've missed the most important thing!

The most important thing is to bring people to Jesus. As we all know, the last thing Jesus said on the face of the earth was:

> Go and make disciples of all nations, baptizing them in the name of the Father and of the Son and of the Holy Spirit, and teaching them to obey everything I have commanded you (Matthew 28:29-20).

Why have we forgotten this lesson? Our whole purpose is to share the good news with the people around us.

You want to work out every day and lose weight and eat healthy and stay in great shape? Fine, that's great, but if you neglect the spreading of the gospel, then you are not living up to your whole purpose of being on this earth.

You want to go downtown and protest injustice and take a stand for the vulnerable? Wonderful! Americans have a long history of protesting injustices, going back to the Boston Tea Party itself, which took place in 1773. It is great to join in solidarity with people who want to make our world a better place.

However, the way you can help people the most ... forever ... is by introducing them to the joy and love of Jesus Christ.

What we have today is a generation of people who are eager to bring others to their social events, but are reluctant to reach out and bring people to the Lord! Wouldn't it be nice if we invited as many people to church as we do to other events such as socials, sports events, coffee time, bowling, or birthday parties? Wouldn't it be nice if we invited all those people to church?

Don't you think our church would thrive more, have more children, have more leaders, have more prayer warriors, have more money to give to the poor, have more hands to serve ... if we had more people?

How are we going to have more people if we don't invite our friends and neighbors? As you've probably heard me say many times before, churches grow in one of two ways: they either have young families who raise children in the church, or else they evangelize the people around them and bring them to church. If you want to grow the church, you basically have to do one of those two things. Or, a third option, is that you can support those who are doing one of those two things.

In today's text, the apostle Paul tells us that he is a kind of chameleon. He is willing to become like an Orthodox Jew in order to bring Orthodox Jews into the church. He's willing to dress like an Orthodox Jew, talk like one, hang out with them, and study the scriptures with them ... if that means he might be able to win them to Jesus.

The great apostle Paul says he became like the weak, so that "he might save some." How did Paul become like the weak? Well, instead of enjoying the life of a prominent rabbi, Paul got out there and learned how to make tents from animal hides. He became a working-class man—a traveling salesman—in order to establish churches all over the Mediterranean world: Spain, Italy, Greece, Turkey, Syria, Israel, and Cyprus.

Paul traveled around and became like the local people, staying in each place several months—sometimes longer—so he could meet people, introduce them to Jesus, and "win as many as possible."

Are you able to become a chameleon for Christ's sake? Are you willing to enter into a group of people with the hope of saving some of them from the corruption of this often-depraved world?

I remember one time, after a Bible Study, a brother in Christ stuck around to ask me a sincere question. He asked me about Christians in India who have chosen to remain in their Hindu communities. In other words, they converted to Jesus, became baptized, and studied their Bible. They prayed to the Lord Jesus Christ. However, they felt like they couldn't leave their community. They would lose all of their social system. He asked me my opinion about whether I thought this was right or wrong.

Here's what I told him. During the early 1700s … you had Protestant missionaries who told their converts in India that they had to leave their Hindu communities if they became Christians. These missionaries, from Europe, thought it was impossible to be a Christian while living in a Hindu village. So, they basically established separate villages for Christian converts. Over time, these villages became known as "villages of refuge" because they were places where Hindu converts could live without being insulted or persecuted by local Hindus. They lived as Christians, yet had to say goodbye to their families and friends.

Here's the problem with such thinking. If someone converted, then they never had any contact again with Hindus in their home villages. They were therefore unable to witness to Christ because they were cast out of their community. The missionaries made these converts leave their Hindu families. But this is the opposite of what Jesus wants.

Jesus wants us to stay in touch with sinners. Jesus doesn't want us to establish little Christian enclaves where we don't have any sinners in our midst. Jesus doesn't want us to establish communes where we escape the world.

Look at what Jesus says, in his famous prayer, in John 17:13–19:

> I am coming to you now, but I say these things while I am still in the world, so that they may have the full measure of my joy within them. I have given them your word and the world has hated them, for they are not of the world any more than I am of the world. My prayer is not that you take them out of the world, but that you protect them from the evil one. They are not of the world, even as I am not of it. Sanctify them by the truth; your word is truth. As you sent me into the world, I have sent them into the world. For them I sanctify myself, that they too may be truly sanctified.

You see that? Jesus does not want us to depart from the world. Whether we are in India or in America. Wherever we go ... the evil one will be there, too. You are called to live "in" the world, but not to become "of" the world. You are to "fit in" to an extent. You are to become a chameleon. Live in this society, function in this society, work in this society, but know that your true citizenship is not of this world.

In Philippians 3:20, Paul tells us that "Our true citizenship is in heaven ... And we eagerly await a Savior from there, the Lord Jesus Christ."

So ... please be a chameleon. Go into your workplace, your communities, your schools, your social circles, and be a chameleon. But do it all in the name of Jesus. And bring some of those people to the church, so that they will enjoy the peace and joy of Jesus Christ. So that they will allow the goodness and righteousness of Christ to dwell in their hearts. You need to "win as many as possible," bringing them to Jesus, so that they will have "hope for eternal life."

Now, this chapter is called "The Tale of Two Chameleons." We've only talked about one chameleon ... and that is the chameleon that you are supposed to be like. You are supposed to change your colors—metaphorically—so you can win people for the Lord.

However, there is another chameleon that you should avoid at all costs. And that is the chameleon that has no true core. That is the person who is a Christian on Sunday, but a mocker or an adulterer on Friday. That is the person who speaks well of people to their face, but slanders them as soon as they leave the room. That is the person who gives money to the poor for show ... they announce it on Instagram. When in fact Jesus tells us that our offerings and our help should be done quietly and secretly.

Sisters, brothers, don't become the bad sort of chameleon. Don't be two-faced. Let us not be part-time Christians. It's easy to be a Christian when the pastor comes to your house for dinner! It's easy to be a Christian on Sundays during church. It's easy to be a Christian when it pays dividends to be a Christian.

But Christ doesn't want part-time disciples. Christ wants your 100% Christian commitment. Christ wants you to follow Him ALL the time. Christ wants your heart. He wants you to be committed to Him.

Otherwise, you become lukewarm. Jesus says something profound about this topic in Revelation 3:14–18:

> These are the words of the Amen, the faithful and true witness, the ruler of God's creation. I know your deeds, that you are neither cold nor hot. I wish you were either one or the other! So, because you are lukewarm—neither hot nor cold—I am about to spit you out of my mouth. You say, 'I am rich; I have acquired wealth and do not need a thing.' But you do not realize that you are wretched, pitiful, poor, blind and naked. I counsel you to buy from me gold refined in the fire, so you can become rich; and white clothes to wear, so you can cover your shameful nakedness; and salve to put on your eyes, so you can see.
>
> Those whom I love I rebuke and discipline. So be earnest and repent. Here I am! I stand at the door and knock. If anyone hears my voice and opens the door, I will come in and eat with that person, and they with me.

The bad chameleon is the person who is a hypocrite. That is what we should avoid at all costs. Jesus is not pleased with part-time disciples. He wants your entire heart. He wants your complete commitment.

But if you have failed, don't give up. Don't get depressed. Jesus says if we have been that kind of chameleon, then we should "repent." He is at the door, knocking, and waiting for us to answer.

The tale of two chameleons is a warning for us. Yes, you should be a chameleon who enters other places in order to bring the light of Christ to the people.

However, don't be the kind of chameleon that stands for nothing. "You've got to take a stand for something, or else you'll fall for anything."

9. Elevate the People Around You

Perhaps one of the most under-emphasized aspects of Jesus's character was his ability to elevate the people around him. He made them better. He took twelve fairly ordinary men—later known as the apostles—and turned them into absolutely extraordinary human beings. The apostles went on to become amazing and accomplished people. They traveled widely and evangelized people far away from Jerusalem. They established churches. They preached the gospel and went through unimaginable hardships in order to push the message of Jesus Christ further.

Jesus's apostles were fishermen, accountants, tax collectors, tent-makers, and men of other professions. Jesus took their talents and turned them into evangelists of the first order. The apostle that features prominently in the biblical account is Paul. Thankfully we have the book of Acts which tells us about his incredible life—as a determined evangelist who was willing to be imprisoned, beaten, whipped, and condemned, all for the sake of spreading the gospel of Jesus Christ.

How did Jesus inspire his followers to such a high degree? How did he "elevate the people around him" to such a level that they became the very best that they could possibly become?

In the gospels, we read about Jesus healing people, forgiving people, advising people, and casting out demons from people. Jesus knew that in order for His message to get out to all the world, he needed followers who were completely devoted to Him. He needed disciples who would carry the torch. Jesus knew His day would probably come prematurely, and it did. He died around 33 years of age—still a young man. He accomplished more in his short life than any man ever has in the history of the world.

But at the heart of Jesus's ministry is His ability to "elevate the people around him."

Our main text for today is found in Mark 5:1-20. It is one of the great stories of the gospels that illustrates Jesus's profound ability to elevate people.

> Jesus and his disciples crossed Lake Galilee and came to shore near the town of Gerasa. When he was getting out of the boat, a man with an evil spirit quickly ran to him from the graveyard where he had been living. No one was able to tie the man up anymore, not even with a chain. He had often been put in chains and leg irons, but he broke the chains and smashed the leg irons. No one could control him. Night and day he was in the graveyard or on the hills, yelling and cutting himself with stones. When the man saw Jesus in the distance, he ran up to him and knelt down. He shouted, "Jesus, Son of God in heaven, what do you want with me? Promise me in God's name that you won't torture

me!" The man said this because Jesus had already told the evil spirit to come out of him.

Jesus asked, "What is your name?"

The man answered, "My name is Legion, because I have 'legions' of evil spirits in me." He then begged Jesus not to send them away.

Over on the hillside, a large herd of pigs was feeding. So the evil spirits begged Jesus, "Send us into those pigs! Let us go into them." Jesus let them go, and they went out of the man and into the pigs. The whole herd of about two thousand pigs rushed down the steep bank into the lake and drowned.

The men taking care of the pigs ran to the town and the farms to spread the news. Then the people came out to see what had happened. When they came to Jesus, they saw the man who had once been full of demons. He was sitting there with his clothes on and in his right mind, and they were terrified.

Everyone who had seen what had happened told about the man and the pigs. Then the people started begging Jesus to leave their part of the country.

When Jesus was getting into the boat, the man begged to go with him. But Jesus would not let him. Instead, he said, "Go home to your family and tell them how much the Lord has done for you and how good he has been to you."

The man went away into the region near the ten cities known as Decapolis and began telling everyone how much Jesus had done for him. Everyone who heard what had happened was amazed.

Everyone was amazed because Jesus was *truly* amazing. He took a scary, demon-possessed man who caused great fear—and he turned that man into a disciple and an evangelist.

When Jesus had an encounter with someone, he made them better. He calmed their spirits, and healed them of whatever was inflicting them. He elevated them. And they were always grateful, wanting to follow Him. Jesus was the ultimate leader—the greatest who has ever walked this earth.

Jesus inspired people. For those of you who are leaders, this should be one of your highest goals—to inspire the people around you. This book about *following Jesus* should help us all to be more inspiring to the people around us. We just have to put these lessons into practice. Don't let them go in one ear and out the other. Do whatever you need to do to ensure the lessons stick.

Do you inspire people? Do you elevate the people around you? Do you elevate your friends? Do you elevate the strangers that you meet on the street, in the grocery stores, or in the businesses that you frequent? Do you elevate the people you talk to on the phone, or the people you communicate with on the internet? Are you elevating the people around you?

In today's society, people are tearing each other down, often without a second thought. Quarreling and mudslinging online is standard fare—it's what many people do in the evenings when resting after work. People lose their temper with others on the phone. Our society is becoming more fractious and polarized by the day. It is almost cliché to recognize this fact.

We can do better than this. Notice how this man we just read about was demon possessed! Not a great guy. The Gospels tell us that he had numerous evil spirits in him.

And what did Jesus give to this man? Jesus drove the evil out of him. Jesus brought clarity of mind to him. Jesus elevated him by giving him his dignity back.

And my guess is that Jesus probably did this for some of you. You were lost, but now you are found. Jesus elevated you. You were caught up in some sin, and Jesus came to you, like He did to Legion, and Jesus helped you. He healed you. And he provided hope and a future for you. Just like He did with me.

I love this passage from the book of James, chapter 1, verse 27:

> Religion that God our Father accepts as pure and faultless is this: to look after orphans and widows in their distress, and to keep oneself from being polluted by the world.

It is very likely that at some point in your life, Jesus helped you to pull yourself out of the pollution of the world. You and I both know it: this world is polluted. And I'm not here referring to climate change or global warming. I am talking about spiritual pollution. It seems people are becoming more and more toxic by the day: fraud, selfishness, distrust, hateful actions, unspeakable immorality, repudiation of religion, a refusal to recognize that there is a God, and so on.

A big part of being a Christian is to remain unpolluted from the world. The world is going to try to pull you down into a fight with someone. The world is going to try to get you to surrender your morality and get you involved in a sinful relationship. The world is going to suck you into fear. The world is going to weigh you down with financial worries, employment worries, and relationship worries. The world is heavy, and will hold you hostage, down on the ground, so that you feel unable to break free.

Like Legion, the demon-possessed man was weighed down with heavy burdens. He had learned to be hated and feared. He learned how to be evil. He knew his role well, and he acted on it. He played the part. He was full of hate and resentment.

But in just a few minutes, after an encounter with Jesus, he was immediately elevated. Jesus set him free from his miserable existence. Jesus delivered him from the demons that were weighing him down for years. Jesus pulled him up from the pollution, and set him in an entirely new direction.

Are you willing to allow Jesus to elevate you?

If you answered yes, then let me ask you a second question … Are you trying to elevate the people around you?

As a disciple of Jesus, you should strive to elevate the people around you. You have the ability to put some goodness into people. You can refuse to allow them to pull you into the pollution of the world. Refuse to be weighed down by fear, discouragement, and hate. Extend hospitality to people. Show kindness in your daily interactions. Be encouraging to people on the internet, rather than adding fuel to the flames. Text Bible verses to the people you know. Help people get away from the sins that keep them weighed down. And keep yourself at a safe distance from worldly pollution.

As James said, pure religion is to keep yourself from being polluted by the world. Instead, you should help people to "shine like stars," as Paul says. Read this wonderful passage of scripture found in Philippians 2:14-16:

> Do everything without grumbling or arguing, so that you may become blameless and pure, children of God without fault in a warped and crooked generation. Then you will shine among them like stars in the sky as you hold firmly to the word of life.

God wants you to shine like stars. Let your light shine. Open up your beautiful heart to people. Paul says that this world is "warped and crooked." That was the case in the year AD 50, and it is still the case in the year 2021. Our world is crooked. There is a bunch of pollution out there that threatens to suck us into its toxic vortex.

But let us resist all of that. Elevate the people around you. Lift them up. Shine like a star. Help drive the demons out of people with your kindness and your sincerity. Pray for evil people. Spread the love of Christ around you, leaving sparkles of God in your wake wherever you go. When you walk around in the grocery store, leave goodness and kindness in your wake. When you talk with someone on the phone, send good vibes to them. When you comment on the internet, bless people, and do not curse them. Don't seek revenge on people; rather, overcome evil with good.

If you take good actions like this, then you will be surprised … you will elevate the people in your life.

And if we can get many others to join with us, then we just might help to elevate our cities, our nation, this world, and even this generation.

10. Love: The Heart of Christianity

In my academic life, I do a lot of teaching about World Religions. It is a course that I teach more than any other. I teach students about many of the world's religions, their history, their texts, their most primary beliefs, and their understanding of the afterlife.

Buddhism's most cherished belief is compassion. Buddhist teachers say that you must have compassion on all people so that you don't contribute to suffering in the world. By having compassion, you minimize the suffering that exists.

Islam's most cherished belief is submission to God. Muslims teach that it is our ultimate duty to fall on our face before God (literally, as they pray in a prostrate position 5 times per day), and submit to His will as laid out in the Quran. Human ethics are important, but nothing is more important than submitting to God, as understood by their most important prophet—Muhammad.

Hindus are most concerned about their homeland, India. Indeed, the word "Hindu" is basically a moniker for "India." The word itself comes from a river in the

Northwest part of the country. Thus, Hinduism's very essence is "Indianness." Hinduism is an ethnic faith. It is first and foremost the religion of the Indian people.

Judaism is similar in this regard. It is the religion of the Jews. Judaism, like Hinduism, is a religion that has a particular people in mind. To be a Jew, in the vast majority of cases, your mother must be a Jew. It is a religion that is passed down through the offspring. Like India, it is also a religion that has a geographical component to it—in this case the nation of Israel. Jews hold a special place in their hearts for the land of Israel. It is the "promised land," and it is rooted deep in the Jewish soul.

Many religions are geographical in nature. Shinto is the religion of the Japanese. Native Americans have a geographical understanding of their religion, as their religion and their land is very closely linked. The same is true for Confucianism. It is the religion of Confucius, but it is so intertwined with the land of China, that it is nearly inconceivable to talk about Confucianism without having a history lesson about China.

Christianity is quite different from all of this – in several aspects. It is a religion that is not linked to a singular geographical place. Christianity began in Jerusalem, but it is a religion for all lands. Christianity was begun by a Jew—specifically Jesus—but it is a religion for all tribes and races and ethnicities. Do you want to know where the most Christians live? Africa! Yes, Africa has more Christians than any other continent. And do you want to know where the second-largest number of

Christians live? Over 90% of Latin Americans profess Jesus as their Savior.

It is interesting that many people tend to equate Christianity with Europe. Yes, there was a time when a whole bunch of Europeans were Christians. Indeed, many of them are still Christians. However, as we just pointed out, Christianity is not linked to a particular soil. It is for all people.

The Christian faith is strongest in Africa, but throughout history it has been the religion for so many people groups, globally. The earliest Christians were all Jews. They were Semitic. The part of the world that has the fastest-expanding population of Christians is in Asia. So let us disregard this notion that Christianity is somehow a European religion. That is not true at all.

Christianity is for Europeans too, of course, but it is also for Jews, Africans, Asians, Native Americans, Pacific Islanders, Latinos, and any other race or tribe or ethnic group in the world.

Thus, Christianity is unique here. It is not tied to land. It is global. It is open for all.

So why have so many people embraced Christianity in the world? After all, it is by far the largest religion in the world. About one out of three people on our planet claims to be a Christian.

The reason Christianity has been so influential, is because of its most central teaching: love. And that is our lesson for this chapter.

Let's look at 1 John 4:7-21:

Dear friends, let us love one another, for love comes from God. Everyone who loves has been born of God and knows God. Whoever does not love does not know God because God is love. This is how God showed his love among us: He sent his one and only Son into the world that we might live through him. This is love: not that we loved God, but that he loved us and sent his Son as an atoning sacrifice for our sins. Dear friends, since God so loved us, we also ought to love one another. No one has ever seen God; but if we love one another, God lives in us and his love is made complete in us.

This is how we know that we live in him and he in us: He has given us of his Spirit. And we have seen and testify that the Father has sent his Son to be the Savior of the world. If anyone acknowledges that Jesus is the Son of God, God lives in them and they in God. And so we know and rely on the love God has for us.

God is love. Whoever lives in love lives in God, and God in them. This is how love is made complete among us so that we will have confidence on the day of judgment: In this world we are like Jesus. There is no fear in love. But perfect love drives out fear because fear has to do with punishment. The one who fears is not made perfect in love.

We love because he first loved us. Whoever claims to love God yet hates a brother or sister is a liar. For whoever does not love their brother and sister, whom they have seen, cannot love God, whom they have not seen. And he has given us this command: Anyone who loves God must also love their brother and sister.

This is the most central teaching of the Christian faith. Let's break the passage down to the most central teachings:

- If we love others, then we can be sure that God is in us.
- God "is" love; thus if we have love in us, then we have God in us.
- If we are "like Jesus", then we live a life of love.
- Love does not fear. Love breeds confidence. Those who live by fear—who put fear first in their lives—are not living according to the principles of love.
- If you hate someone, then you are violating God's most central command. Hate is the opposite of God.
- If you hate others, then the love of God is clearly not living inside of you.

I don't know about you, but this is very challenging teaching for me. However, none of this is surprising when you read the Bible. Jesus spelled this all out with great clarity.

For example, let us look at Matthew 22:36-40:

> "Teacher, which is the greatest commandment in the Law?"
>
> Jesus replied: "'Love the Lord your God with all your heart and with all your soul and with all your mind.' This is the first and greatest commandment. And the second is like it: 'Love your neighbor as

yourself.' All the Law and the Prophets hang on
these two commandments."

Jesus could not have been clearer. As a Christian living on this earth, your first duty is to love God, who is in Heaven. Your second duty is to love your neighbor as much as you would even love yourself. Everything else is a footnote.

And as we all know, the apostle Paul wrote what is perhaps the most beautiful passage in all the world's literature when he described love in 1 Corinthians 13. The passage is often read at weddings: Love is patient, love is kind, it does not envy, it does not boast, it is not proud, etc.

Let's read the prelude to the famous "love chapter" in the Bible, located at First Corinthians 13:1-4. Before Paul defines the concept of Christian love in that chapter, he tells us of the value of love on the scale of Christian priorities. Here's what he wrote:

> If I speak in the tongues of men or of angels, but do not have love, I am only a resounding gong or a clanging cymbal. If I have the gift of prophecy and can fathom all mysteries and all knowledge, and if I have a faith that can move mountains, but do not have love, I am nothing. If I give all I possess to the poor and give over my body to hardship that I may boast, but do not have love, I gain nothing.

So, what is so distinctive about Christianity? What is our unique contribution to the world of religion? It is love. That is what is central to Christian faith. When it comes to the Christian faith, nothing else takes priority over the concept of love.

So, what does this mean for you and me? Well, that is perhaps the most important question a Christian can ask. Love makes all the difference in a person. Love is what turns a person of hate and vengeance into a person of tenderness and forgiveness. Love is what turns relationships around, making them thrive again. Love is what happens to you when you try to find the best in people, rather than looking for their faults.

Love is what causes you to extend mercy to people. Instead of holding grudges, you allow yourself to forgive someone who has done you wrong. Love is what does that. Nothing else can accomplish what love can accomplish.

If your marriage is falling apart, love can rescue it and help your relationship to thrive once again. If you had a falling-out with somebody, love can restore the relationship once again because it forces you to become humble, willing to do whatever you need to do to achieve reconciliation.

Love can change you in powerful ways. Do you have someone you hate or resent? Love can change that. Love can cause you to soften your heart. It can cause you to shed tears of joy when you realize you forgive the person who wronged you. Love does not keep a record of wrongs; rather, it causes you to let those things go. You forgive others their trespasses, just as God forgave your trespasses.

Only love can do this, sisters and brothers. Only love can help you change your outlook against your former employer who wronged you. Only love can make you look into the eyes of someone who betrayed you, and suddenly have compassion on them—and see their dignity. Only love can transform your heart from one of bitterness to one of grace.

My friends, you are a member of the religion of love. No other religion in the world emphasizes love like this. It is a distinctively Christian trait. If you live a life of love, then you are well on your way to living the life of Jesus. If you love other people, even your enemies, then you have moved closer to "following Jesus."

This book is about "Following Jesus," but let us make no mistake here—nothing is as important to the Christian faith as is love. The apostle Paul even says that love is greater than faith. He says in 1 Cor. 13:13: "These three things remain: Faith, Hope, and Love, but the greatest of these is love."

So, as you go about your week, I want to encourage you to throw away your bitterness, and replace it with Christ's love. Let go of the resentment you have been carrying, and replace it with love for that person. If you see injustice in the world, try not to hate the one who brought the injustice. You should love them, and try to transform them into being a disciple of Jesus if you can. The best thing you can do for them, and the best thing you can do for yourself, is to forgive them.

We are members of the religion that excels in love. The whole point of Christianity is that you will turn to God—the God of Love. That you will allow this same God to soften your heart so that you might release the bitterness within your heart. That you might trust Him to transform you into a person who lives their life with profound love.

And, ultimately, if you achieve that goal, you will become a bit more like God. You will become a person of love. Because God is love.

11. The Problem with Secrets

Did you hear about the preacher who decided to take a Sunday off? He called up the elders and told them he would need to miss the next Sunday because he had something very important that he needed to attend to. He certainly didn't tell the elders that the real reason he took off that Sunday was so he could play a round of golf. The elders informed the church that the preacher wouldn't be preaching that Sunday as he had some very important business to attend to, so the church would have to find someone else to deliver the sermon that day.

So, then the preacher scheduled himself a tee time at a very fine golf course located about half an hour away. He chose a golf course where nobody would recognize him, as he didn't want to have to explain himself.

So, the preacher stepped up to the first tee box and hit a beautiful drive. The ball went up and up and then a big gust of wind came along and pushed that ball 420 yards, way up onto the green. And wouldn't you know it … the ball kept rolling and rolling and eventually went right into the hole. It was a hole in one! He had never hit a hole in one in his life.

But then it dawned on him. He could not tell anyone about his hole-in-one because it would ruin his secret that he had skipped church just to play golf!

Secrets usually don't pay off. Jesus calls us to live lives that are open, honest, and transparent. God calls us to walk in the light, not in the dark places. Jesus lived his life in the open. He avoided secrets, as secretive living leads to confusion.

Now, don't get me wrong. There are times when we need to communicate confidentially. If you ever want to talk with your pastor, I am pretty sure they would keep it confidential. Indeed, the laws of our nation protect Christian ministers, since it is common for Christians to open up to their priest or pastor about marital troubles, struggles, conflict with others, or other deeply personal matters. And Christian clergy fully realize that this is a sacred trust. People need to open up about these things sometimes without others knowing.

However, these are the exceptions to the rule. Most of our lives should be lived with openness, honesty, and transparency.

Secrets come in many packages. People have secretive relationships. People have certain sides to themselves that they shelter from the rest of the world. They have financial difficulties that they don't want to discuss. Some have issues from their past that they would rather not reveal.

Overall, we could say that secrets have many downsides. They can cause you to become nervous, having to keep track of who knows and who doesn't know. In keeping secrets, you must hide aspects of yourself. You try to keep people away from certain aspects of you. You become closed off in certain areas of your life.

Secrets can drain us of our energy. One of the big reasons we keep secrets is because we are fearful. We are afraid we will be found out. We are afraid we might lose a relationship. We are afraid somebody might not accept us anymore. Or we are afraid that something might be taken from us if the secret gets exposed. So, it puts us into a fearful and nervous state.

Sometimes, we don't want to be found out, so we even change our personality, trying to intentionally lead people away from the secret. We may choose to confuse people so they don't see us clearly and authentically.

Sometimes we share secrets about other people. This can be very troubling. We think to ourselves that we can malign this person when so-and-so is not around. Or we can run down this person to that person, and so on. However, this is a self-destructive way to conduct our social life. It comes with guilt. We are told clearly in the Bible that we should not slander people, or gossip about them; it violates many tenets of our faith.

When we gossip and slander, we actually undermine ourselves because if we are capable of gossiping about or slandering one person, then the person we are talking with realizes we are the type of person who gossips and slanders. It is likely we will lose credibility in their eyes.

The best policy is to talk about people positively, or else not at all. Sometimes it is good to imagine that person in the room. Think to yourself, "How would I talk about that person if they were sitting right here."

Again, there are times when you may need to open up to a counselor or a pastor or a close friend. But a general rule is to be very, very cautious about the possibility of slandering, smearing, or gossiping. This is ungodly behavior, and it could potentially backfire. It is a secretive approach to communication that is unbecoming of one who tries to walk openly in the light of Christ.

Some psychological studies have shown that secrets often lead to fatigue. They can lead to shame, guilt, and embarrassment. They can cause social isolation. A good study showed that college students who kept secrets from people eventually found themselves socially isolated because of the guilt they had regarding the secrets they were keeping. They said certain things and did certain things that they were ashamed of, and thus they became neurotic or anxious around the people that might be offended by their words or actions. The study showed that all of that secret-keeping takes a toll on the mind.[1]

Another study showed that keeping secrets causes people to perform at lower levels. They took two groups of people. One group was told to think about non-secret information while they put together puzzles. The other group was told to think about the consequences of revealing a particular secret in their life, and put together a puzzle. As you might expect, the people who were thinking about the consequences of their se-

---

[1] https://www.psychologytoday.com/us/blog/experimentations/201901/the-secrets-you-keep-are-hurting-you-heres-how#:~:text=Beyond%20that%2C%20keeping%20secrets%20may,and%20satisfaction%20with%20one's%20life.

crets performed much worse. They were focused on fear, anxiety, and outcomes of spilling the beans. Whereas the others just freely put together the puzzles.

Perhaps this is all predictable, but it is telling, nonetheless. When we have secrets that we are withholding from the people around us, we have to think harder and measure consequences. No one can think clearly when they are consumed with fear or retaliation. We perform much better in our jobs, relationships, and even mundane tasks when we are clear-headed, authentic, and free of concern.

What the psychologists will tell you is that you need a few confidantes in your life. You need a close friend who is like a brother or sister. Proverbs 18:24 says, "One who has unreliable friends soon comes to ruin, but there is a friend who sticks closer than a brother."

You need close confidantes. You need a pastor or a therapist. You need a few people in your life with whom you can share your secrets. If you are married, then you need iron trust with your spouse. These people that you have deep trust with will help you to escape the neurotic, often self-defeating behavior that comes with keeping secrets.

It is also important just to realize that secrets can be draining. Live openly, with integrity, and without having to keep a lid on your secrets.

And let me restate: there are things you must keep to yourself. What if your close friend opens up to you about their marital problems? Definitely, you should keep those things quiet. However, you need to help your friend process that information because eventually, it probably needs to come to light.

Same with yourself. If you have a secret, you don't need to go to the opposite extreme and post it on Reddit. No, you probably need to begin by opening up to a family member or close friend. That way, you can start lifting the lid on that secret, and start shedding some light on a corner of your life that was previously hidden.

For example, if you are drinking alcohol in secret all the time, there is the Alcoholics Anonymous program that encourages openness. You are asked to introduce yourself by saying, "My name is David, and I'm an alcoholic."

Why do you think they do that? They do that because people often keep this information secret until it begins to cause problems in their lives. It spills over in their work life, in their relationships, perhaps even in the form of drunk-driving.

Let me share with you three important passages about secrets in the Bible. The first is from 1 John 1:5-7,

> This is the message we have heard from him and proclaim to you that God is light, and in him is no darkness at all. If we say we have fellowship with him while we walk in darkness, we lie and do not practice the truth. But if we walk in the light, as he is in the light, we have fellowship with one another, and the blood of Jesus his Son cleanses us from all sin. If we say we have no sin, we deceive ourselves, and the truth is not in us. If we confess our sins, he is faithful and just to forgive us our sins and to cleanse us from all unrighteousness.

The second passage is Ephesians 5:8-18:

> At one time, you were in the dark. But now you are in the light because of what the Lord has done. Live like children of the light. The light produces what is completely good, right and true. Find out what pleases the Lord. Have nothing to do with the acts of darkness. They don't produce anything good. Show what they are really like. It is shameful even to talk about what people who don't obey do in secret. But everything the light shines on can be seen. And everything that the light shines on becomes a light. That is why it is said,
>
> "Wake up, sleeper.
> Rise from the dead
> Then Christ will shine on you."
>
> So be very careful how you live. Do not live like people who aren't wise. Live like people who are wise. Make the most of every opportunity. The days are evil. So don't be foolish. Instead, understand what the Lord wants. Don't fill yourself up with wine. Getting drunk will lead to wild living. Instead, be filled with the Holy Spirit.

And, finally, we have an important word from Jesus himself, in Matthew 10:26-28,

> So do not be afraid of them, for there is nothing concealed that will not be disclosed, or hidden that will not be made known. What I tell you in the dark, speak in the daylight; what is whispered in your ear, proclaim from the rooftops. Do not be afraid of those who kill the body but cannot kill the soul. Rather, be afraid of the One who can destroy both soul and body in hell.

Let's choose to live in the light. Let's live in the light, as He is in the light. Let's use discretion when we talk about others. Let's conduct ourselves with integrity.

I once heard a preacher give the definition of integrity, and it went like this: "Integrity is being the same in the dark as you are in the light."

Let's read Proverbs 28:13:

> Whoever conceals their sins does not prosper, but the one who confesses and renounces them finds mercy.

Let's confess our sins, let's be discriminating about how we talk about people, and let us live as children of the light.

May God bless you as you live a life of openness and accountability. Live without guilt or shame. Try to avoid secrets, and try to live openly with the people you love and trust.

12. Go Out and Spread the Good News

I research in the area of Christianity in India. I travel to India regularly to study Indian Christianity, connect with Indian churches, preach the Word, and collaborate with Indian colleagues.

Recently, I was having a conversation with some Indian scholars via email. We were discussing the issue of whether to spread the gospel in India right now.

Perhaps that sounds like a weird thing to discuss … Of course, we should spread the gospel in India, right? But, what if you converted to Christianity and then became an outcaste? What if you lost your job for converting to Christ? What if your children were to experience humiliation, shame, and persecution for becoming a Christian?

These are difficult questions. And churches have come to different conclusions about how to answer them.

In order to help you understand the situation in India today, I should let you know that right now in India, there is a fundamentalist Hindu government in charge of the nation. They uphold Hinduism as the "true" religion, and they denigrate all other religions. Since India is about 80% Hindu, they enjoy landslide victories. They have been in power, virtually uncontested, since 2014. There seems to be no end in sight for this political party.

As a foreigner, I have to be careful. Westerners are monitored these days when traveling in India. We are carefully vetted at the border, and we have to make sure we don't get onto the radar of the local police. And evangelism will definitely get you onto their radar! Big time! I once attended a baptism in India that required us to drive way out into the countryside, to an isolated stretch of the river, to avoid the watchful eyes of the government, or the watchful gaze of local Hindus who might spill the beans if given the chance.

It can be dangerous to get baptized in India, but it can be even more dangerous *to baptize* someone in India right now. There are major risks involved.

How should Christians respond to this situation? What is to be done?

There are four ways that the Indian churches are responding to the issue of whether to evangelize or not.

1. Some churches defy the law. We can call this group the Zealots. Indian law tends to say that you should not convert people. But these zealous Christians are motivated by Peter in Acts 5:27–29: The apostles were brought in and made to appear before the Sanhedrin to be questioned by the high priest. "We gave you strict orders not to teach in

Jesus's name," he said. "Yet you have filled Jerusalem with your teaching and are determined to make us guilty of this man's blood." Peter and the other apostles replied: "We must obey God rather than human beings!"

These Indian Christians say, "We must follow Christ and not the human laws." However, these Christians must deal with grave consequences if they get caught. They can be harassed for following Christ's command to "Go out into all the world and preach the gospel." These churches are usually demonized in the media as being insensitive to local culture. They are considered foolish by the media for trying to convert other people without regard for the social consequences.

2. The second group of Christians is much more cautious, but they still think it is important to spread the gospel. These are the Evangelicals. These people realize it is a difficult and sensitive situation. However, they also realize that it is more important to follow God. So, they come up with a way to obey the law publicly, yet to carry on evangelism privately. These are the Christians who are motivated by Paul's command in 1 Corinthians 9:19-23: "Though I am free and belong to no one, I have made myself a slave to everyone, to win as many as possible. To the Jews I became like a Jew, to win the Jews. To those under the law I became like one under the law (though I myself am

not under the law), so as to win those under the law. To those not having the law I became like one not having the law (though I am not free from God's law but am under Christ's law), so as to win those not having the law. To the weak I became weak, to win the weak. I have become all things to all people so that by all possible means I might save some. I do all this for the sake of the gospel, that I may share in its blessings."

These Christians choose to "become all things." When they are with Hindus, out in public, they act like good citizens. However, when they are in a private conversation, they might try to evangelize someone with whom they have developed a friendship. They use discretion, and are very careful. They realize they could be betrayed. But they go about their lives, "becoming all things to all people" in order to "save some" with the good news of Jesus Christ.

3. The third group can be called the Progressives. They are Christian people, but they have decided that evangelism is not the way to go. It will make you run afoul of the government, which might bring shame to the Christian community. This is the group that thinks the best way to live as a Christian in India is to do good works such as medical care, social improvement, education, and speaking out against social injustice. These people often rise up to good positions in India because they are usually very educated. They are often

economically secure, so they have too much to lose. These Christians often have good jobs. And to get caught evangelizing might not only bring shame, but it could actually mean you lose your job, lose your influence, and lose your good name. These Christians have made the calculated decision to speak with actions, not with words of evangelism. They are motivated by the words of the prophet Micah, in Micah 6:8: "*What does the Lord require of you? To act justly and to love mercy and to walk humbly with your God.*" They have counted the cost, and have come to the decision that they will spread God's love, but will not preach the entire gospel. They realize that it would be better to serve their society in the name of justice than to attach the name of Jesus to it. These people will tell you openly, "We do not evangelize. We don't believe in evangelizing because we realize that the consequences will be terrible for those who might convert to Christianity."

So, in a way, these Christians are being selfless. They are trying to protect others while still serving them with acts of kindness, with providing food, with medical care, with education, and with many other acts of justice and mercy.

4. The fourth group of Christians is what we call Pluralists. These are Christians who have come to the decision that God loves all people, and God will save good people regardless of their particular theological beliefs. These people would never, ever

evangelize another person, as that could be misconstrued as coercion. Why would you try to get someone to leave their social group, leave their religion, leave their friends, leave their temple, and deal with social isolation from their family? Why would you want to inflict that kind of social and psychological damage onto another person that you barely know? This group values the saying from Peter in Acts 10:34-35, where Peter says, "God does not show favoritism, but accepts from every nation the one who fears him and does what is right." They argue that God can be as pleased with a good Hindu as He is with a good Christian. These people will say that it doesn't matter what religion you're a part of. What matters is that you are a good person. Whether you are a Hindu, a Muslim, a Jew, or a Buddhist, you just need to stay in that religion and be the best Hindu or Buddhist that you can be.

These people get angry when you talk about evangelism or conversion. They are totally opposed to evangelism. "Live and let live" is their mantra. You should leave people alone when it comes to something as profound and all-encompassing as religion. Preaching the gospel, trying to get people to become Christian is—in their view—a malicious, even violent act. They will often focus on God's love, saying, "God loves everyone. Every single person. Regardless of your beliefs." What these people fail to see, however, is that when Peter spoke the above words, he mentioned Jesus in the very next breath (Acts 10:34-38): Then Peter began to speak: "I now realize how true it is that God does not show favoritism but accepts from every nation the one who fears him and does what is right. You know the message God sent to the people of Israel, announcing the good news of peace through Jesus Christ, who is Lord of all. You know what has happened throughout the province of Judea, beginning in Galilee after the baptism that John preached—how God anointed Jesus of Nazareth with the Holy Spirit and power, and how he went around doing good and healing all who were under the power of the devil because God was with him."

Yes, Peter said that God accepts people from every nation, but Peter also speaks of people needing to turn to Jesus Christ, "who is Lord of all." Peter was not saying that Jesus was a "take it or leave it proposition." Indeed, Peter himself gave his life for Jesus. Peter knew the consequences of denying Jesus. And we all know that Peter did deny Jesus, but he later repented of his sin and came back to Christ. Probably many times in his life, Peter had heard Jesus's words in Matthew 10:32-33: "So everyone who acknowledges me before men, I also will acknowledge before my Father who is in heaven, but whoever denies me before men, I also will deny before my Father who is in heaven."

The choice is yours. Are you going to be a Zealot, an Evangelical, a Progressive, or a Pluralist?

Let me be clear here. I think we need to preach the gospel. I also believe that you have to be savvy about how you do it. I have seen zealous evangelists run through the streets screaming, "Repent, for the kingdom of God is near!" I am not going to judge those people, but I will say that I, personally, have chosen a different way to evangelize.

So, in sum, I think whether you evangelize openly or privately, you need to be evangelizing. As a Christian, I must evangelize. I must share my faith. I would not feel obedient to the Great Commission in Matthew 28:19-20 if I neglected to preach the gospel:

> Therefore, go and make disciples of all
> nations, baptizing them in the name of the Father
> and of the Son and of the Holy Spirit, and
> teaching them to obey everything I have command-
> ed you. And surely I am with you always, to the
> very end of the age.

Those words are pretty unambiguous. "Go and make disciples." "Baptize them." "Explain the Trinity to them —that God is Father, Son, and Holy Spirit." "Teach them to obey the teachings of Jesus."

These are nonnegotiable. We need to be doing these things if we choose to "Follow Jesus."

You don't live in India. You probably live in the United States of America. And each one of us must decide whether or not we are going to share Christ with those around us.

13. God and Mammon

Have you ever heard of the restaurant called "French Laundry," in Napa Valley, just north of San Francisco? It is considered one of the top 50 restaurants in the world according to one website.

If you have ever eaten at this restaurant, then may I advise you to give a nice donation to your church? To eat at this restaurant costs between $350 and $850 per person. Let's just round it off at $600 per person. If I took my family of six, I'd need to be prepared to drop around $4000 for a meal there. With tax and tip ... well, there goes my savings.

In Malibu, we have a restaurant called "Nobu." It is a place where you can catch celebrity sightings virtually any time, day or night. After reading about the restaurants in northern California, I guess eating out in Malibu is a bargain. A meal at Nobu, on the beach near my house, costs between $100 and $300, depending on whether you eat appetizers and order a bottle of wine.

My family and I drive by Nobu every time we head to McDonald's—where I can feed my entire family for $30. Those $5 and $6 meal deals have kept the Daughrity family well-fed through the years ... and we get to keep our savings.

With such high prices, you'd think these expensive restaurants would be struggling to get business. After all, the global economy is not exactly humming. But so many people seem happy to drop a grand or two in order to enjoy a really nice plate of food. An article I read states: "... fine dining restaurants are seeing higher demand than ever."

We are a society swimming in money. I'll never forget when I bought my son his first nice mountain bicycle (more than just a Walmart special). We bought it used from a guy down in Orange County who wanted to upgrade to the next level, so he was getting rid of his old mountain bike—the one we wanted. He said he was selling his old one because he had his eye on another bike that was going to cost him $12,000. Yes, that's right, $12,000. In fact, I asked for clarification. I asked, "Do you mean $1200?" No, he reiterated. The price of a top-flight bike that has everything he wants would cost him $12,000.

In my worldview, $12,000 will get you a car! It might be a few years old, but you can get a decent one for that amount.

This chapter is about God and Mammon. What is mammon, you ask? Mammon is the Aramaic word for "riches" or "wealth." Jesus spoke the language of Aramaic. And in the Aramaic culture, they had a pre-Christian god called "Mammon" that represented human wealth. Thus, for these reasons, the Bible translators in the past—such as the King James Version—used the word "mammon" much of the time when they translated this passage. However, the meaning of the word is simply "wealth, money, or riches."

You have probably heard this word *mammon* in the gospels, specifically in the Sermon on the Mount, in Matthew 6:19-24.

> Do not store up for yourselves treasures on earth, where moths and vermin destroy, and where thieves break in and steal. But store up for yourselves treasures in heaven, where moths and vermin do not destroy, and where thieves do not break in and steal. For where your treasure is, there your heart will be also.
>
> The eye is the lamp of the body. If your eyes are healthy, your whole body will be full of light. But if your eyes are unhealthy, your whole body will be full of darkness. If then the light within you is darkness, how great is that darkness!
>
> No one can serve two masters. Either you will hate the one and love the other, or you will be devoted to the one and despise the other. You cannot serve both God and money (mammon).

This is a challenging passage to preach in American society. I realize that very few of us are truly rich—like Elon Musk or Jeff Bezos or Mark Zuckerberg—but compared to most of the world, we are doing pretty well. The U.S. is a nation that is truly blessed with plenty of food, homes, goods and services, respectable salaries, and benefits. Most of us have leisure time every week—we don't have to work our fingers to the bone.

When we travel to other places that are part of the developing world, it can be striking what much of the world goes without. Several of our members travel to Mexico occasionally to build houses for families. My own children told me about the scarcity that exists there. It was good for them to see that, and to understand that scarcity better—a scarcity that is common in the developing world.

When I travel to India, I am struck by the fact that three generations commonly live in one house. I have often witnessed a working father who puts his entire family of four onto his motorcycle to go somewhere. I see vast numbers of people who have extremely low-paying jobs. I see children working in restaurants.

It can be challenging for those of us living in America to understand these things. You and I inhabit a world that most south Asians cannot even fathom. Again, I'm not saying all of us are rich. We're not, when comparing ourselves to upper-class Americans. But when we compare ourselves to the vast majority of people in Asia, Africa, and Latin America—we are living very comfortable lives.

And you want to know what is really amazing about our successes here in the U.S.? The amazing thing is that it wasn't long ago that Americans—our ancestors—struggled mightily to eke out a living. My grandfather and grandmother met while hoeing cotton. They struggled through the Great Depression, suffering in ways that you and I will probably never fully understand. It wasn't very long ago that America was a place where people really struggled to eat.

I am reminded of the movie *Cinderella Man*. It's an excellent film about a former boxer in the Great Depression who has to start fighting again to keep bread on the table, as boxing is the only thing he's qualified to do. He tries getting a job on the docks, but they don't have anything to offer. He starts training to start boxing again, although he's actually too old at that stage of his life. There is one scene where he is about to get himself a glass of milk, but he looks down at his hungry kids and realizes they must take priority. He only has a little bit of milk, so in order to make the milk go a bit further, he has to dilute it with water so they can each have a glass. He and his wife went without. It is a powerful scene.

So, what are we to do about serving "God and money?" Why did Jesus say you cannot serve both God and money?

I think this passage from Matthew is teaching us that money can ruin us if we're not careful. It can become like a God to us. The apostle Paul says the following about money, in I Timothy 6:6-10 (TLB):

> Do you want to be truly rich? You already are if you are happy and good. After all, we didn't bring any money with us when we came into the world, and we can't carry away a single penny when we die. So we should be well satisfied without money if we have enough food and clothing. But people who long to be rich soon begin to do all kinds of wrong things to get money, things that hurt them and make them evil-minded and finally send them to hell itself. For the love of money is the first step toward all kinds of sin. Some people have even turned

away from God because of their love for it, and as a
result have pierced themselves with many sorrows.

Did you catch that? The love of money is the first step towards all kinds of evil behavior. It can lead you away from God. As Jesus said, "You cannot serve both God and money." Loving money too much can lead you to into "many sorrows." You came into the world without money, and you'll leave the world without money, so don't long for it as if it is absolutely necessary.

There is, of course, much good that comes out of money. You can help people with it. You can build a church with it. You can support a missionary with it. You can pay for your kids' education with it. Of course, money can be a good thing!

In fact, money itself is not the problem. It is "the love of money" that is a problem. The Bible teaches that work is important to do, so you can make money, buy food, and feed your family. Listen to what the apostle Paul says in 2 Thessalonians 3:10-12:

> While we were with you, we used to tell you,
> "Whoever refuses to work is not allowed to eat."
>
> We say this because we hear that there are some
> people among you who live lazy lives and who do
> nothing except meddle in other people's business.
> In the name of the Lord Jesus Christ, we command
> these people and warn them to lead orderly lives
> and work to earn their own living.

All work that is honest and dignified deserves a wage. It is important to work hard and earn a paycheck. It is important that we not "muzzle the ox while it is treading out the grain." If a man or woman works, he or she should enjoy the fruits of their labor.

In 1 Timothy 5:17-18, Paul speaks specifically on the issue of those people who work and lead and preach in the church. He says:

> The elders who direct the affairs of the church well are worthy of double honor, especially those whose work is preaching and teaching. For Scripture says, "Do not muzzle an ox while it is treading out the grain," and "The worker deserves his wages."

Work hard. Earn your pay. Make money for your family or for your own livelihood. But don't start falling in love with it, like Gollum did in the Lord of the Rings. He says, "My precious" every time he looks at the ring. He starts falling in love with it. And he gets possessive of it. And it destroys him eventually.

The Bible tells us that it is important to work hard. The problem comes when you start being overly possessive and greedy. The problem is when you become a slave to your money: "You cannot serve both God and money."

So, you might ask, what are the practical lessons here? This book is about "following Jesus." What must we do if we are going to be faithful to the gospel, and faithful to the tenets of our faith?

There are three clear lessons that come out of these scriptures:

1. The money you earn is a gift from God.

2. Use your gifts in a godly way. Help others, support your family, and bless others.

3. If you start feeling too attached to your money, then watch out. That means your money is starting to become your master.

If you make a good salary, then don't be ashamed! Be thankful to God, and use it for good! Use it for God.

If you are feeling tight-fisted, then do some soul-searching, and take action. Find someone in need and help them. Use your money to build up the Kingdom of God. Employ someone. Find a way to help people with that money.

Finally, let us all realize that money can destroy us. So many people have been destroyed by the love of money.

Earn it. Use it. Make some. Give some away. Bless people with it. Buy yourself some food – okay, maybe not an $850 meal at French Laundry – but be proud of the fact that you worked hard, and now it's time to eat.

Money is a gift from God. And with all gifts from God – they work best when you offer them back to Him. God is the source of all gifts – and we must always remember that.

We close this chapter with a famous parable that Jesus told (Luke 12:13-21):

> Someone in the crowd said to him, "Teacher, tell my brother to divide the inheritance with me."
>
> Jesus replied, "Man, who appointed me a judge or an arbiter between you?" Then he said to them,

"Watch out! Be on your guard against all kinds of greed; life does not consist in an abundance of possessions."

And he told them this parable: "The ground of a certain rich man yielded an abundant harvest. He thought to himself, 'What shall I do? I have no place to store my crops.'"

Then he said, 'This is what I'll do. I will tear down my barns and build bigger ones, and there I will store my surplus grain. And I'll say to myself, "You have plenty of grain laid up for many years. Take life easy; eat, drink and be merry."'

But God said to him, 'You fool! This very night, your life will be demanded from you. Then who will get what you have prepared for yourself?'

This is how it will be with whoever stores up things for themselves but is not rich toward God.

14. Jesus Taught Us to Pray

I am always refreshed when I pray. I feel refreshed when I hear others pray. The only complaint I have about prayer is that I don't do it enough.

Prayer is the lifeblood of the Christian life, just as it was the lifeblood of Jesus's life and ministry. Jesus was sent from heaven to earth, but while on earth he kept his communication with God going strong. Just as if you go on a long trip to the other side of the world, but you have a cell phone, and you have a good cell phone plan. You are able to keep up with your family while traveling. This has been a big part of my life, as I have traveled for missions, for research, and for university work. However, whenever I am in some far away country, I still get to talk with my wife Sunde and the kids and my Mom through email, phone, and social media.

Similarly, when Jesus came to our earth, he kept his lifeline going with God. He prayed to God often. Any time Jesus was about to engage on a major task, such as launching his ministry, or before he was about to be crucified ... in those extremely important moments, Jesus prayed hard. He reached out to God. And the gospel writers noted this. They saw Jesus praying intensely at these important times.

For example, the Gospel of Luke states in chapter 6, verses 12-13:

> One of those days, Jesus went out to a mountainside to pray, and spent the night praying to God. When morning came, he called his disciples to him and chose twelve of them, whom he also designated as apostles.

So, we have Jesus praying before he chooses his apostles. Part of the Christian life is praying before we make decisions, just as Jesus did in his life, over and over again.

Many of you will be making decisions, important decisions, in the near future. Where to go to college. Where to retire. Whether to apply to a different job. Where to get treatment for an illness. Whether to date a particular person. When to have children. These are important moments in life. And we all should be praying about our personal circumstances. We all should be praying that God will lead us in the right direction, that God would provide for us, that God will point us in the direction of new opportunities, and that God will direct our paths.

Jesus's life was a life of prayer, and if there is nothing else that you gain from this chapter, I hope it is this: that you should often pray because Jesus prayed often. Indeed, the apostle Paul says in 1 Thessalonians: "Rejoice always, pray without ceasing, give thanks in all circumstances; for this is the will of God in Christ Jesus for you."

Let us remember that the biblical understanding of prayer is that we do it at important times in our lives. But it is also the biblical view that we should pray without ceasing. Let us remember to keep in touch with God throughout our days. When you are at work, keep the prayers going. When you are driving on the highways, keep the prayers going. When you are walking around your neighborhood, reach out to God. When you are relaxing at night, send some prayers up to God. Prayer is what Jesus did, and prayer is clearly what his disciples thought he expected them to do.

As we all know, Jesus prayed, and he prayed often. But he actually talked a lot *about* prayer. You get the sense that prayer was frequently on His mind. Remember, like when you travel across the world, prayer is your lifeline back home. Prayer is how we stay connected to our Father, who is in Heaven.

Here is one of Jesus's most important teachings about prayer. It is found in Matthew 6:5-8:

> And when you pray, do not be like the hypocrites, for they love to pray standing in the synagogues and on the street corners to be seen by others. Truly, I tell you, they have received their reward in full. But when you pray, go into your room, close the door and pray to your Father, who is unseen. Then your Father, who sees what is done in secret, will reward you. And when you pray, do not keep on babbling like pagans, for they think they will be heard because of their many words. Do not be like them, for your Father knows what you need before you ask him.

What does this important passage of scripture teach us? What we have here is extremely important. It is the Son of God, teaching us about prayer. Let us analyze that teaching here. I want to bring to light several points that come out of this teaching:

1. Let's not try to show off in front of people when we pray. There is a time for public prayer, of course. But prayer is not about eloquence, according to Jesus. It is not something we do in order to impress others. We don't pray to show our intelligence or our wisdom. We pray in order to make contact with our Heavenly Father, seeking His will in our lives. We pray because we love God. As a community, we need His presence, and we turn to Him as a community—to express our faithfulness to Him.

2. If we want to be seen by God, we need to pray privately, in secret, when no one else is watching. That is the kind of prayer that is powerful and effective. Jesus tells us plainly here, when we pray privately, God will reward us. God will give us rewards. Think about that? Do you want blessings? What does the Bible say you should do? The Bible says that if you want rewards, you should go to God privately, and pray to Him. "… and He will reward you." That should be quite a promise for us. We have it, straight from Jesus, that when we pray privately, God will provide us with rewards.

3. Prayer is not supposed to be a big complicated affair. We don't have to impress God. We don't have to persuade Him with our arguments. God knows what we need. We don't need to use a lot of words when we pray. God appreciates the person who turns to Him with direct, deliberate, sincere prayers. He wants us to simply put it out there. We cannot manipulate God, as He is far superior to that kind of nonsense. God sees right through us, and our motives. What we need to do is to seek God out and simply tell Him what we would like Him to do.

God is not a genie. We have a mistaken understanding of God if we think he is here for our demands. Rather, we are here for God's demands. We are God's children, but we are also God's servants. We are here on this earth to do His will. We are workers in the vineyard of the Lord.

This is important to get right in our heads. It is not about us. It is about aligning our will with the will of the Master—the Lord of all. We pray because it is our attempt to align our will with the Lord's will.

And when we pray often—unceasingly—we become more like God. We become changed. For example, Jesus often tells us to pray for our enemies. Why? Why would you want to pray for your enemies? They're the ones who are making life miserable for us, right?

Jesus says, in Matthew 5:43-46:

> You have heard that it was said, 'Love your neighbor and hate your enemy.' But I tell you, love your

> enemies and pray for those who persecute you, that you may be children of your Father in heaven. He causes his sun to rise on the evil and the good, and sends rain on the righteous and the unrighteous. If you love those who love you, what reward will you get?

We pray for our enemies because it is actually good for us. We begin to see them as children of God. It is very hard to hate someone who is on your constant prayer list. It is hard to resent them forever. Eventually, your vision of them will start to change. Your perception of them will begin to align with God's perception of them. They are sinners. They messed up. They mistreated you. But they are redeemable. God cares about them. And God is hopeful that they will come around and start behaving.

When we pray, we get a bit of God's perspective on humanity. God is our Father. If you are a parent, you'll understand this lesson. As parents, we might discipline our kids for, say, burping at the table during dinner, or forgetting to turn the light off after leaving a room. But we certainly don't remain angry at them for these mistakes. Even when they hurt us ... we forgive them. Similarly, we make mistakes all the time. But God doesn't declare us guilty when we come to Him. He forgives us. He wants the best for us. And, let us keep in mind, God wants the best for your enemy, too. So that's why it is important to pray for your enemy. God wants to share His goodness with them, too.

If your enemy is living in outright rebellion against God, then God will deal with them. Just like God dealt with me, and with you, when we wandered off His path from time to time in the past. God chastised us. He disciplined us. So perhaps your enemy will come back around. Pray for them. Try to see them like God sees them. Go to your room, shut the door, and pray for your enemies. This is what Jesus commands you to do, explicitly.

I want to challenge you to build more prayer time into your life. There are endless ways to pray. You can pray the scriptures. You can pray whatever comes to your mind. You can pray to God during those intense, decisive times in your life. You can pray to God through song. You can pray with friends. You can pray collectively with your church.

But one thing you cannot do ... you cannot live the Christian life very well without prayer. It is crucial. It is the lifeblood. Prayer for the Christian has been compared to oxygen for the body. It is something you do, as when you breathe.

I want to encourage you to take advantage of the awards that are awaiting you. Jesus said you will receive rewards when you pray. We'd be foolish not to try to gain some of these rewards for ourselves, and for the people we are praying for. We should pray that God would heal people. We should pray for our nation and our leaders. We should pray that God would help us in our jobs. We should pray that God will provide us with what we need. We should pray that God will give us that big breakthrough we've been wanting.

God will decide on what to do. So, you and I don't need to worry about that. God is not going to harm us when we approach Him with requests. God says He won't give us a poisonous snake if we ask for fish to eat. He may not answer us the way we expected, but He won't harm us.

As we follow Jesus, let's remember to pray. Prayer should be a constant thing we do. Pray to God also when your head hits the pillow at night. Pray to Him the first thing in the morning when your eyes open.

He is our Father. And He desires to hear from us often.

15. Listen, With Empathy

Let's define that word, "empathy." I looked it up, and here is the best definition I found: "Empathy is the ability to understand and share the feelings of another."

It reminds me of the famous prayer attributed to St. Francis, where he says, "Lord, help me to seek first to understand, and then to be understood."

I don't like to talk about politics much. However, that does not mean that I don't care about politics. I do care, I just don't think they should play a role in public ministry. For example, when I preach, I try not to lean to the left or to the right. Rather, I try to proclaim the Word of God in simple terms that all people can understand. I try to make the Gospel more comprehensible by using analogies and illustrations that we can all relate to. Jesus was the master at that method. I try to connect with what is going on in the world around us. Like the theologian Karl Barth famously said, preachers should have the Bible in one hand and the newspaper in the other.

And if we read the "paper" (which typically means something from the internet these days) we will probably find that our society has become rather uncivil much of the time. People aren't listening very well these days. People tune each other out. Or worse: they scream at each other. They hurl insults. They roam the streets, seething with anger, sometimes even causing destruction to cars, buildings, and people. We have entered a strange moment in our nation's history, and I don't think our local and national governments know what to do about it.

But I can tell you what we need to do as Christians. We need to look to God. We need to pull out our Bibles, and search the scriptures for how God wants us to behave. We need to throw ourselves before God and ask for forgiveness. We need to pray for our leaders, pray for our enemies, and pray for ourselves—that God might protect us and keep us from descending into incivility in our dealings with each other.

We should "Listen, with empathy." Let's listen to people. And not merely listen to them, but try to understand where they're coming from. Let's try to get behind the words that they may be screaming, and commit to giving them a fair hearing. Even if someone disagrees with us, let us learn how to be civil, to remain quiet and humble while they talk. And let us learn how to have grace on them, and remember to love them, no matter what.

All of us know "the love chapter" in the Bible, which is 1 Corinthians 13. Some of you had that passage of scripture read at your wedding. I'm not going to read the entire chapter, but I do want to point to two verses in that chapter: verse 1 and verse 13.

In verse 1, the apostle Paul says, "If I could speak all the languages of the earth and of angels, but didn't love others, I would only be a noisy gong or a clanging cymbal."

In verse 13, Paul says, "And now these three remain: faith, hope, and love. But the greatest of these is love."

So far, so good. I think this much is clear: whatever you do, wherever you go; however, you decide to live your life ... if you don't have love, you are mistaken.

Secondly, love is the most excellent thing in all the world ... even more than faith and hope. Love is the greatest command, and it is the one thing that you must do if you are a Christian. The whole point of Christianity comes down to love. If you neglect love, then you neglect the Christian faith.

And one major way that we show love to others is by having empathy on them. We listen to them. We have compassion on people.

One time during a Bible Study I was leading, I challenged the attendees to look at each other with love in their eyes. In Mark 10:21, the gospel describes a scene where Jesus is talking to a rich man, and it says, "*Jesus looked at him and loved him.*"

What I took from this passage is that Jesus had empathy on this rich young man. Jesus looked at him with love in his heart. And I encouraged the attendees at the Bible Study to do the same. Whenever we look at someone, let's try to think loving thoughts about them. There are psychological studies that show how difficult it is to think negative thoughts when you are smiling. And what I'm asking you to do is similar. Whenever you look at people, try to think loving thoughts about them.

Look at the cashier with love in your heart. Look at people in your workplace while having love in your heart for them. Look at your spouse, and think loving thoughts about them. Don't think about how someone annoys you. Don't think about how someone wronged you. Don't think about how someone may have it better than you. Look at them and try to think loving, caring, compassionate thoughts.

Sometimes it helps to remember that everyone was a child once, with parents who loved them and raised them. All of us who are adults are actually just grown-up children. We all have or did have parents who loved us.

Jesus did this kind of thing. When he was face to face with an adulterous woman, rather than condemning her, he had compassion on her. He loved her. He thought caring thoughts about her.

When Jesus came face to face with a demon possessed man in Luke 8, Jesus listened to him. Jesus let that man talk. And then Jesus healed him of his demon-possession. Jesus got past the fear and intimidation that probably came naturally to whomever talked with a deranged man like this. Jesus refused to cower down in fear. Jesus stood firm, listened to the demon-possessed man, and then found a way to help him.

When Peter betrayed Jesus, still our Lord had compassion on him. We read about this scene in John 21:15-21. Keep in mind that Peter has just betrayed Jesus, and denied even knowing Jesus. And then Jesus gets crucified. After resurrecting, Jesus finds a time to talk with Peter alone. Jesus still had faith in Peter, even though Peter had pretty much committed the worst sin a person can commit: he completely denied Jesus.

Jesus, however, spoke with Peter. He reinstated Peter. He looked at him with love. He had compassion on him and forgave him. And Jesus even asked Peter to continue to represent His cause as an apostle. Jesus then recommissioned Peter as an apostle and as a missionary.

It was an extraordinary scene because the natural, instinctive reaction is to return fire with fire. Not many of us forgive people who turn against us, who bear false witness against us, or just ignore us. We tend not to have much compassion in those situations.

Jesus, however, had empathy. He probably understood that the reason Peter denied Jesus is because he was scared that he might get crucified too.

What does all of this say to you and me? Well, let me conclude this chapter with some biblical advice that will hopefully make it clear what you can do to improve in this area of your life:

1. You can look at people with eyes of love. You can think loving thoughts about them when you look at them. When you look at someone on a screen, think compassionate thoughts about them. When you look at your spouse, think lovingly about him or her. Think about what they have done to help you in your life. Think about their dignity. Think about how much you love them. Look at them with

love and compassion. You can convey tremendous compassion to people by how you look at them.

2. Be present to people in your life. Don't just walk by people. Stop for a moment and try to engage them. Ask them how they are doing. Look at them and pause and say hello. Be meaningful with the people that God happens to put into your life. Just take a few minutes to say hello. Maybe strike up a conversation with the lady at the cash register. When your spouse or child enters the room, ask them how they are doing. And be present when they respond. Be present when they return your efforts to engage them.

3. Listen to people. Don't cut them off when they talk. Give people the benefit of the doubt. Loving people means listening carefully to them, understanding their needs and their emotions. It is much more important to listen to somebody than to talk to somebody. Seek to understand where they are coming from. This practice will help you to have more compassion. Be a great listener. Try to comprehend why people are hurting, or angry, or depressed. Don't feel the need to fix them. Just listen and have empathy.

4. Be tenderhearted towards people. Listen to this wonderful verse from 1 Peter 3:8: "Sympathize with each other. Love each other as brothers and sisters. Be tenderhearted, and keep a humble attitude." Don't allow your anger to get the best of

you. Don't lose your patience with people. Be tenderhearted. Look at them lovingly, and deal with them lovingly.

Finally, as we all know, "Hurt people hurt people." Who are the people out there who are hurting people? It is the same people who have been hurt. That's right. "Hurt people hurt people."

The only solution to this cycle of hurting is to not hurt people. Be tender with the people around you … including your family! Sometimes we are the least compassionate with the people who are closest to us.

"Listen, with empathy." Let's be empathetic, and to look at others with love in our hearts, and with love in our eyes.

16. When to take other opinions seriously

In life, there are two different tendencies: 1. The tendency to take people too seriously; and 2. The tendency to not take people seriously enough.

In Ecclesiastes 7:21, we read this verse:

> Do not pay attention to every word people say,
> or you may hear your servant cursing you—
> for you know in your heart
> that many times you yourself have cursed others.

Let's focus on that passage for just a moment because I think many of us probably take the opinions of others too seriously. We hear that someone talks bad about us, and we get really, really hurt. We hear that someone perhaps doesn't think too highly of us, and we feel deeply insulted. Or we hear that someone doesn't approve of something we did, and we get spiteful. Sometimes we even want to get vengeance, so we go around slandering them, spreading bad news about them, even speaking against them to their face.

This should not be. We should do our part to keep peace between ourselves and others. As Paul says in

Romans 12:18, "If it is possible, as far as it depends on you, live at peace with everyone."

But notice that Paul says, "As far as it depends on you." There are times when people are simply going to sin against you, and there is not much you can do about it. Somebody will get jealous of you. Or they'll disagree with you on something. Or they'll want to put you in your place. And if someone gets aggressive or hostile against you ... well ... that is their choice. Unfortunately, or fortunately, we live in a free society. People have the freedom to treat us poorly, to say things against us, to disrespect us—even to our face.

But you and I must stay above all of that. We should not let their opinions affect us to the point that we start behaving like them!

Let's face it, some people are foolish. The Bible talks about foolishness a lot, especially in the book of Proverbs. Some people are fools. They are sinful. They don't have good motives. Those kinds of people are out there. And they'll try to undermine you sometimes. But you've got to rise above all of that, and stick to your principles, and do what you know to be the right thing.

Social media has helped us in ways, but it has also been destructive to people, especially people who have grown up with the internet. People long for approval from their "friends" and "followers" on social media pages. People desperately want their phone to make that sound when they receive a "like." Scientists tell us that we get a hit of dopamine every time we get a notification.

Studies have shown that people who get addicted to cell phones are often like those lab rats who get addicted to a little bit of the drug in the test tube that they put into the cage. In the case of social media, that little "ding" gives us a brief "high" that we long to hear again and again. We become like those little lab rats, and we go back hundreds of times a day to get the "ding"—the dopamine.

But the Bible says that we should not fall into this mousetrap. And it is a trap. Again, let's look at that Ecclesiastes verse (7:21): "Do not pay attention to everything people say."

People are very fickle animals. One day, they'll be kind and generous, and the next day they'll speak ill of you to their friends. You have to rise above all of this. Don't get sucked into it. It can be painful, but the best approach is to just drop it.

Social media is a place where you can become extremely discouraged. People get destroyed in their spirit when they see people mocking them, or making fun of them. But what is so surprising is that everybody basically keeps going back for more dopamine.

The internet is a brutal place. All you have to do is look on social media feed to see people getting into fights every day, insulting each other, disapproving of each other, calling each other out, cursing against one another. It's a brutal world online, and you've got to use discretion about what to talk about online.

Even an innocent post can become the target of someone's ridicule. There are fools out there. And they are just lying in wait for someone to lambast.

But here's where it gets tricky. We all want approval. We all want to be liked and respected. We all want people to agree with us, and to value what we say. But social media is not the place to seek out that approval. In fact, there are a lot of people whom you should simply disregard because they are happy to insult you or to otherwise try to put you in your place. We should try to avoid these people.

And now the second part of the chapter: there are some people we don't tend to take seriously enough.

We need to give more attention to the people who vocally affirm us. We need to pay attention to the people who express love for us, or solidarity with us. We need to pay attention to the affirming voices that help us along in this life.

Proverbs 17:17 says, "A friend loves at all times, and a brother is born for a time of adversity." The people we need to listen to are our "real" friends—the people who invest in our well-being. We need to develop close relationships with those people who care deeply about our soul. We need to stick close to those people who are going to love us "at all times."

You need to listen to the voices that encourage you. Listen to the voices that build you up. Because if you listen to the mouths of fools, you could endanger yourself. They can rob you of your peace. They can hurt you deeply. Fools can bring you down. Listen to these passages from Proverbs 15:

> A gentle answer turns away wrath,
> but a harsh word stirs up anger.

The tongue of the wise adorns knowledge,
  but the mouth of the fool gushes folly.

The soothing tongue is a tree of life,
  but a perverse tongue crushes the spirit.

The lips of the wise spread knowledge,
  but the hearts of fools are not upright.

The Lord detests the way of the wicked,
  but he loves those who pursue righteousness.

Mockers resent correction,
  so they avoid the wise.

A happy heart makes the face cheerful,
  but heartache crushes the spirit.

The discerning heart seeks knowledge,
  but the mouth of a fool feeds on folly.

A hot-tempered person stirs up conflict,
  but the one who is patient calms a quarrel.

The heart of the righteous weighs its answers,
  but the mouth of the wicked gushes evil.

According to the book of Proverbs, there are two major categories out there: the fools and the righteous. The fool blabs his or her mouth, committing sins, and "gushing out evil." The righteous person makes people cheerful, makes people calm, helps people to understand more by giving them knowledge.

Notice what the fool does. She or he:

1. Stirs up anger;

2. Crushes people's spirits (mentioned twice, in vv. 4, 13)

3. Stirs up conflict;

4. Gushes evil.

So which voices are you and me going to listen to? I hope we listen to the people who are righteous ... and let us keep a good distance from the fools. When it comes to fools, you should wear a mask, and use social distancing. (Remember that?)

Proverbs 26:4 says, "Don't answer fools when they speak foolishly, or you will be just like them."

Proverbs 26:21 says, "Just as charcoal and wood keep a fire going, a quarrelsome person keeps an argument going."

There is one opinion in particular that you should take very seriously. And that is the opinion of Jesus. His voice is the one you should listen to, and follow.

Listen to what Jesus says in John 10:27-30:

> My sheep listen to my voice; I know them, and they follow me. I give them eternal life, and they shall never perish; no one will snatch them out of my hand. My Father, who has given them to me, is greater than all; no one can snatch them out of my Father's hand. I and the Father are one.

We must listen to somebody's voice. There are some people who listen to nobody, and they are fools. They have no accountability. They feel like they can bully and hurt others, and gossip without any repercussions.

But you ... don't live your life that way. You need to listen to the voice of Jesus. Listen to your Bible. Listen to what you hear in church. Listen to the encouragement from your friends—the people who truly care about you. Listen to the people who have time for you, and want to be with you.

Don't listen to the fools out there who want to drag you down. All they want to do is to kill the spirit, and destroy your joy. You have to tune them out. And socially distance yourself from them.

In sum, there are some voices you should listen to. And there are other voices you should completely disregard.

You will be mentally happy and spiritually fulfilled if you listen to the positive voices. And you will be a lot better off if you shut out the voices of fools in your life.

A key part of following Jesus is listening to Him and His people ... not the fools.

17. Neither Do I Condemn You

The Bible is full of wonderful stories and lessons about grace. And there is one story about grace and forgiveness that is unforgettable. It is the story of the woman caught in the act of adultery.

John 8:1-11

> Jesus went up to the Mount of Olives.
>
> At dawn, he appeared again in the temple courts, where all the people gathered around him, and he sat down to teach them. The teachers of the law and the Pharisees brought in a woman caught in adultery. They made her stand before the group and said to Jesus, "Teacher, this woman was caught in the act of adultery. In the Law Moses commanded us to stone such women. Now what do you say?" They were using this question as a trap, in order to have a basis for accusing him.
>
> But Jesus bent down and started to write on the ground with his finger. When they kept on questioning him, he straightened up and said to them, "Let any one of you who is without sin be the first

> to throw a stone at her." Again he stooped down and wrote on the ground.
>
> At this, those who heard began to go away one at a time, the older ones first, until only Jesus was left, with the woman still standing there. Jesus straightened up and asked her, "Woman, where are they? Has no one condemned you?"
>
> "No one, sir," she said.
>
> "Then neither do I condemn you," Jesus declared. "Go now and leave your life of sin."

We don't really need much commentary after reading that powerful piece of scripture. I'm tempted to just leave it there and let us all ponder that beautiful story, that incredible act of understanding and mercy from the King of Kings and Lord of Lords.

However, let's investigate this scripture a bit and see if we can pull some lessons out of it, applying it to our lives.

First, what was it about this reading that impacted you?

I think there are about four different angles for reading this scripture. Let's look at those angles.

First, perhaps you read this story from the perspective of the woman. Have you ever been caught—cold—in a sin? Perhaps you committed a sin that brought great shame upon you or upon your life, and you felt you had no escape. People found out about your sin, and they talked about you and your bad decision.

Most sins are secret. Most sins are committed by you alone, or by you in the presence of just one or two people. Maybe you cursed at someone. Maybe you fretted all through the night, rather than allowing the Lord to handle your concerns. Maybe you committed a sin of the flesh, like this woman did.

Whatever the case, when you read this story, perhaps you identified with the woman who got caught. You realized that you did something wrong, and you could not turn back the hands of time. The sin was committed.

Perhaps you have sins in your past that are not confessed. And you have guilt in your heart. You are haunted by shame.

Here's the question for you: How does God feel about that? How does Jesus feel about the fact that you sinned?

Here's what he says, "Neither do I condemn you."

Jesus wants to heal you and help you … not condemn you. Jesus wants to comfort you. He wants to take away your shame. He wants to give you your joy back, so you don't descend further into the spiral of sin and shame. If you confess your sin to Him, then he is faithful and will remove your sin. Here's what 1 John 1:9 says, "If we confess our sins, he is faithful and just and will forgive us our sins and purify us from all unrighteousness."

To be sure, the Lord wants you to "leave your life of sin," as he says in this passage, but he does not stand there pointing at you.

That's what *they* did. And that's precisely what Jesus did *not* do.

Who are "they?" *They* are the accusers. The scribes and Pharisees. They are the hypocrites. They are the ones who point at you. "Sinner!" they say. They are the ones who are ready to accuse you and attack you because you made a mistake. "They" are the ones who want to hurt you. They want to rob you of your self-respect. "They" want to ruin you in the eyes of the community. "They" want you to pay the price for your sin. "Suffer!" That's what they want. They want us to suffer in shame and guilt when we sin.

They want you to feel the pain. They want you to hurt and agonize. Yes, they want to silence you.

They lift up stones. They are going to hurl metaphorical stones (like insults and accusations) at you. This is how they did it in the days of the Bible. For the sin of adultery, they threw stones at people and killed them.

"They" are the ones who are eager to point out all the wrongs you did, but they are ever so reluctant to point out their own sins. Here's what Jesus says, about "them" in Matthew 7:5. "You hypocrite! First remove the log from your own eye. Then you will see clearly to remove the piece of sawdust from another believer's eye."

Are you one of "them"? Are you quick to rush in to accuse another person for something they did, but slow to advertise your own sins? Are you the person who wants to tear down "sinners" because they are so awful and sinful? Are you the one who wants to mete out the punishment, instead of leaving it to God?

In the New Testament, Satan is known as "the accuser." Satan loves to accuse. He tries to embarrass people, destroy their reputation, and call people out in public. Satan loves to haunt you … he loves to humiliate you.

The men standing around in the text are like little Satans. They are accusers. They long to accuse this woman publicly, and then kill her in broad daylight. They delight in destruction. They plan to throw their stones at this woman. They are sickening. They are so evil. They are satanic.

Here's what Jesus says about Satan and his techniques, in John 10:10: "The thief comes only to steal and kill and destroy; I have come that they may have life, and have it to the full."

Don't be like "them." Don't thrive on condemnation. Don't long for the humiliation of others. Don't glory in someone else's shame. Let us not relish the thought of degrading someone publicly. That is a path to self-condemnation.

Third, there is a character in this story that you may have missed. Read carefully the second verse in this passage. There it is: "all the people." We are told that "all the people" gathered around Jesus early in the morning. They were planning to hear Jesus teach there in the Temple courts in Jerusalem, when suddenly the Pharisees loudly and triumphantly bring their "catch of the day" – this woman – and they throw her down in front of Jesus. It absolutely ruined the scene. Jesus was about to teach … people were excited to hear him.

And here come the accusers, pulling the adulteress out of the place she was in, hauling her across the town, and then forcing her to the ground in front of Jesus, there at the temple courts in Jerusalem.

But I want to ask you if you read that story from the perspective of "all the people." Maybe you are in that crowd. You are watching someone get humiliated. Perhaps you are the one reading the insults ... online ... getting sucked in to a horrific and humiliating scene that is literally causing trauma in someone's life.

Are you in that crowd of "all the people?" Where are you sitting as you watch these bullies mishandle and mistreat this woman? Are you slightly relieved, just thankful that it is not you this time? Or are you sitting there watching, just hoping that someone else will speak up for her and help her? Are you one of those people in the crowd who stand and do nothing while a grave injustice is occurring? Are we perhaps part of "them?"

Let me encourage you to run to the woman. Cover her nakedness with your coat. Confront the accusers. Stand up to the bullies on behalf of the innocent. Woe to us if we stand idly by while such a horrible scene unfolds right in front of our faces.

Are we standing there filming the scene with our phones? Are we making sure that we're going to catch this so we can post it online? Or are we going to help a fellow sinner? Are we going to try to save this woman from such debilitating shame? Perhaps we are one of those who will come to the rescue of a person who needs forgiveness and protection from the mob?

Fourth, and finally, wherever you are in that scene ... I want you to put yourself into the sandals of Jesus. Stand up for the sinner. Be strong and courageous. Defend the sinner without subjecting yourself to the sin. Yes, indeed, love the sinner ... but hate the sin.

Jesus deliberates in this beautiful story. He bends down to write in the sand, while they kept questioning him. He refused to answer quickly ... because he was thinking.

Then, in a composed manner, Jesus straightened up and said, "Let any of you who is without sin to be the first to throw a stone at her."

Silence...

They knew their own hearts. They, too, had sinned. They, too, had experienced mercy. And they, too, had some humanity within them.

And ... eventually ... they all started walking away.

I hope we can all try to be like Jesus whenever we are confronted by sin. Let us not throw stones. Let us not stand there, recording the situation on our phones, passively.

Let us be like Jesus. We should confront the accusers. But let us not turn the tables on them and condemn them. I love how Jesus simply gets them to think. "Are you sinless? Okay, then you have earned the right to condemn this woman. If you are sinless, you can get us started here in hurling stones at this woman."

Jesus, however, calls them to search inside their own hearts.

Search inside your own heart. Are you an accuser? Or are you a sinner? Are you the one who was thrown down onto the dirt, humiliated, because you failed? Are you the one who gave in to the temptation and did something wrong? Are you a person in the crowd who stood there and did nothing? Are you the person who could have helped, but chose not to defend the weak?

Where are you in this scene? Please search your heart. Where are you?

Jesus tells you … "Neither do I condemn you."

Friends, you have sinned. All of us have. And there is probably some shame there.

But Jesus tells you in no uncertain terms, "Neither do I condemn you."

And let us not forget Jesus's parting words to the woman: "Go now, and leave your life of sin."

Go on. Rise up. Put your self-respect back on. Be proud of who you are. Don't cave in to that shame. God put you onto this earth for a reason. And what is your reason for being here? It is to be the hands and feet of Jesus.

So go now … and leave your life of sin. You are not condemned. You have been set free from your sin. You can be proud of yourself. You can be thankful that you have a God who removes your sin, rather than piles it on top of you.

You have a God who stood up and faced Satan, and defeated him. You have nothing to fear. You are safe. And you can walk away from here with joy in your heart. Jesus has saved you. Go now, and be free from worry.

Go now, in peace. You are forgiven. That is the message of the gospel.

18. Therefore, Keep Watch

Are we living in the last days? Do you think the end times are coming soon?

In the Gospel of Matthew, chapter 24, we read about many signs that will accompany the end of days. Jesus tells us that there is coming a day when (Matt. 24:30-31):

> There will appear the sign of the Son of Man in heaven. And all the peoples of the earth will mourn when they see the Son of Man coming in the clouds of heaven, with power and great glory. And he will send his angels with a loud trumpet call, and they will gather his elect from the four winds, from one end of the heavens to the other.

However, Jesus warns, there will be some troublesome signs before that great day comes. In Matthew 24, Jesus says the following will occur in the last days:

- Many leaders will claim to be Christian (vss. 4-5) and will claim openly that they are the Messiah.

- There will be "wars and rumors of wars" (v. 6). In fact, Jesus says, these wars "must happen" during the end times.

- There will be terrible strife in the world, as "nation will rise against nation, and kingdom against kingdom" (v. 7).

- We will have famines ... there will not be enough food (v. 7).

- There will be earthquakes (v. 7).

- Jesus tells us that these are all "birth pains" and they are inevitable (v. 8).

- Followers of Jesus (v. 9) will be "handed over to be persecuted and put to death."

- Jesus says his followers (v. 9) will be "hated by all nations" because we put our faith in Him.

- Many people (v. 10) will actually apostatize. They will "turn away from the faith and will betray and hate each other." Yes, put bluntly, Christians will rat on each other. They will turn each other in to the authorities ... and they will abandon the faith as they do it. They will completely jettison the church, and their own personal faith.

- Jesus tells us that many false prophets will appear during the last days (v. 11), and many people will be deceived by them.

- Jesus tells us that during the last days, there will be a noticeable "increase of wickedness" (v. 12). Perhaps you've noticed that?

- We are told that people's love for each other will "grow cold." People will harden in their hearts towards each other (v. 12).

So, what are we to do about all of this? Isn't this pretty disastrous and frightening to all of us? The last days sound horrible. Shouldn't we start panicking?

Well, there again, Jesus gives us the advice we need during those last days. He says in v. 6, "See to it that you are not alarmed. ... Such things must happen, but the end is still to come."

Jesus exhorts us (v. 13) to "stand firm to the end, and you will be saved." He tells us that the gospel will be preached despite all of the persecution, despite the natural disasters happening around us, and despite the chaos that must occur. It will be like "birth pains" (v. 8). These things must happen for the end to come about.

But God's servants will still preach (v. 14). To all nations we will preach, even at the risk of our lives. I plan to keep preaching amidst the chaos that is sure to divide the people, the nations, and the world at large. I plan to keep preaching "the gospel of the Kingdom of God" (v. 14). We must keep preaching God's Word despite the pressures that will come upon our people and upon our world.

Jesus says in v. 21, "For there will be great distress, unequaled from the beginning of the world until now—and never to be equaled again."

And after a period of tribulation, Jesus says in verse 29, "The sun will be darkened. The moon will not give its light. The stars will fall from the sky. And the heavenly bodies will be shaken."

Then, a great thing will happen. Jesus tells us that after the heavenly bodies are shaken, "There will appear the sign of the Son of Man, and he will come from the east" (v. 27). He will come with power, and with the angels, and with a loud trumpet. And the angels will "gather Christ's elect" (v. 31) from all over the world.

We know that Christians are today scattered, literally, all over the world: Asia, Africa, Latin America, the Pacific, Eastern and Western Europe, North America, and the Middle East. The Christians will be gathered from all over the earth.

It is going to be chaotic, violent, and painful. But we know that Jesus will indeed come. Many people wonder if we are perhaps entering those "last days."

- We have pandemics that come upon us every few years: AIDS, Avian flu, COVID-19.

- Some fear that our once prosperous way of life could collapse.

- Nations are declaring war on each other, as we've seen in several pockets in Africa, in the Middle East, and in Eastern Europe.

- The great persecution against Christians could potentially happen soon … maybe it is already starting to happen.

- Perhaps the United States may turn on itself. We already are a nation divided in several ways. Perhaps we will soon experience a division the likes of which we have never seen before.

But before we get too zealous in our declaration that the end times are near, we must pay heed to Jesus's words in Matthew 24:36. He says, "But about the day or hour no one knows, not even the angels in heaven, nor the Son, but only the Father."

Did you catch that? We read that when Jesus walked the earth, not even he knew the final day, nor the hour. Only God the Father had that information.

We are not privy to when. We are, however, privy to the fact that it will happen, and it will be devastating. Jesus compares it to "the days of Noah," when tens of thousands of people were struck down by God for their wickedness and their lack of belief, for their lack of obedience (v. 38).

Jesus tells us people were eating and drinking and having weddings in those days. But then, suddenly, disaster struck. People were drowned by the thousands, and there was nowhere to turn for safety. They had turned their backs on God and on righteousness, and the wrath of God came in the form of a flood.

Jesus says,

> The flood came and took them all away. That is how it will be at the coming of the Son of Man. Two men will be in the field; one will be taken and the other left. Two women will be grinding with a hand mill; one will be taken and the other left (vss. 39-41).

How are we to respond to all of this?

Jesus says (vss. 42, 44), "Therefore keep watch because you do not know on what day your Lord will come. ... You must be ready, because the Son of Man will come at an hour when you do not expect him."

Jesus tells us that at the Second Coming, the faithful servant is the one who is remaining obedient to God throughout all of these trials (vss. 45-46). But for the person who has descended into wickedness, who "beats others" and "drinks with the drunkards" (v. 49), they will experience great surprise at the Second Coming of the Master. They will be caught off guard. They will be "cut to pieces," and will then be assigned a place with the unrighteous, "where there will be weeping and gnashing of teeth" (v. 51).

In light of all of this, my dear sisters and brothers ... what are we to do?

I think Jesus's commands are fairly clear here, but let's spell them out.

- We are told to remain faithful ... knowing that the master will come back at an hour no one expects.

- We are told to "be ready." To "keep watch." We are to wait for Christ's return ... expectantly.

- We trust that Jesus will come back with His angels and will put an end to the suffering of His people. We will experience release from the persecutions that we are undergoing.

- We are told to be careful about following false prophets. Jesus is our only Master. Other voices are false, and dangerous, and we must stay faithful to Jesus alone.

- We are told to remain faithful, even if persecution comes.

- We are told to keep our love alive, to keep our hearts warm, and to remain loyal to each other, as so many people will rise up with brutality and will turn against each other. They will not have warmth and love in their hearts. But we must not join those people, for they are headed for death, destruction, and towards hell itself.

- We are told to be careful not to be deceived. False messiahs will rise up.

- We are told to remain calm. Jesus tells us that we should not become alarmed (v. 6), since "such things must happen."

Are we entering the "birth pains" of the end times? I think it is possible. But I just don't know. Jesus tells us that no one knows. It would be foolish for a follower of Christ to claim that they know we are entering the last days. Jesus himself said he doesn't even know when that last day will come. "Only the Father" knows (v. 36).

So, if Jesus didn't even know, and if the angels don't know, then I can assure you that no human being knows. Let us not listen to the people who claim that they know the day or the hour. They obviously don't know, as they are not privy to this information.

I think the question for you and me is … How are we going to respond to the chaos going on around us?

The way we respond is informed by what we do know. We know God will reward us for our faithfulness. We know chaos and war and natural catastrophes will happen, so we should not be surprised by anything, frankly. Desperate times will come.

But Jesus tells us that we should remain calm, because He is coming back to save his own. You and I will be united with Jesus and his angels. He will gather us from the four winds, wherever we may be. And we will be welcomed into the Promised Land, into the new heaven and into the new earth, where there will be no suffering and no tears.

When you are persecuted, as a Christian, I want to encourage you to remain steadfast. Remain calm. Realize that many Christians have suffered for their faith for 2000 years. Your job is to remain faithful. Don't get involved in the wars and in the rumors of wars. Don't turn against people, rather, "love your enemies" as your Master Jesus commanded you to do. When people rise up against each other, you remain poised. Know that these things must happen.

Whether these are the final days of humanity, we just don't know. Let's put our hope and trust in the things we do know rather than in the things we are told we will never know. Let us put our energy into serving our Master, Jesus Christ, waiting for Him, looking to the East, listening for the Trumpet, and watching for the angels to appear.

Jesus Christ, the Messiah, is coming back to save us. This is our shared hope as Christians.

Do not fear. Just keep watch. For He is coming soon.

"Come quickly, Lord Jesus."

19. How to mess up your life: Be Selfish

In this chapter, we will learn how to mess up a life. Doesn't that sound inspiring?

Well, the truth of the matter is that we all get ourselves into messes, and they can be difficult to clean up.

Cleaning up a mess that your pet made, or that your child made … these kinds of messes pale in comparison to a true mess … when you really mess up your life.

Let me share with you a personal story. When I was a late teenager, 17, 18, and 19 years old, I made a real mess of my life. I don't have to go into all of the details, but suffice it to say that I was not in a good place. I had lost motivation. I was living for myself, and had become extremely selfish. My relationship with the Lord declined precipitously, just at a time when I needed Him most. I was neglecting the Bible, and my church life was less than robust.

One thing I did have going for me, however. I somehow realized that I needed to get into a Christian environment, so I enrolled at Lubbock Christian University, a Christian school about 90 miles from my little New

Mexico town. But, as often happens, I found the wrong crowd. It's strange how that happens. Just when we need the Lord the most, we end up getting drawn to the wrong sort of people. And then the mess that we are in just gets messier.

And then one night, I just realized that I had had enough. I reached the end of my rope. I was running on empty, realizing that my life was headed nowhere fast.

So I went into the dormitory, and I asked a group of guys who were playing pool, "Do any of you know someone who is a real serious Christian?" They paused and looked at each other. I am sure they realized that I was looking a bit distraught, perhaps a bit disoriented.

One of them answered, "Sure, there is a Christian guy named John Williamson up on the second floor, in room 209. Go knock on his door. He's a serious Christian." I had met John before, but I didn't know him well at all.

I did not know it at the time, but God was leading me, by the power of the Holy Spirit, up to John's room. As I look back on that night, I am reminded of the saying from Jesus in Matthew 7:7-8:

> Ask and it will be given to you; seek, and you will find; knock and the door will be opened to you. For everyone who asks receives; the one who seeks finds; and to the one who knocks, the door will be opened.

My life was an unholy mess ... but one thing I still had ... I still had the capacity to knock. I knew down in my heart that my life needed to change. And God led me to the door of "a serious Christian" named John

Williamson, in room 209, of Johnson Hall, at Lubbock Christian University.

Unbeknownst to me, John Williamson kept a journal, and he wrote about that night in his journal. And he sent this entry to me years later. It was about the evening that I stopped by his dorm room. I'll read that entry to you now:

> Tuesday, November 17, 1992: Last night ... an interesting event took place. A guy I know came to me wanting to talk. He said he was "referred" to come and talk to me. I didn't ask who. He shared with me some sins in his life that were controlling him. He was broken up over what was taking place in his life. He said how he knew what he was doing was wrong, but he kept finding himself in the same situations over and over again. As we talked and looked at some scriptures I believe I saw a truly repentant heart. It has been a long time since I've seen someone with a heart like this brother in Christ. As he prayed, he bawled – it makes me think of the Psalm 51:17, "The sacrifices of God are a broken spirit; a broken and a contrite heart. O God, you will not despise." Today when I talked with him, he said he was feeling good. The type of good meaning rest. He was at peace with himself and my soul is glad in seeing it.

I had made a total mess of my life by that point. And I needed help. I had become totally selfish, with almost no active connection to God, and it was ruining me. I am reminded of James 3:16, "Wherever there is jealousy and selfish ambition, there you will find disorder and evil of every kind."

The Bible has many, many warnings about what happens to your life when you fall into selfishness. You end up mired in sin because we were not made to be selfish. We were made to seek after the interests of others ahead of our own.

Here are some helpful scriptures about selfishness, and the dangers of living the selfish life:

- Philippians 2:4: "Let each of you look not only to his own interests, but also to the interests of others."

- 2 Timothy 3:2-4: "For people will become lovers of self, lovers of money, proud, arrogant, abusive, disobedient to their parents, ungrateful, unholy, heartless, unappeasable, slanderous, without self-control, brutal, not loving good, treacherous, reckless, swollen with conceit, lovers of pleasure rather than lovers of God."

- 1 Corinthians 10:24, "Let no one seek his own good, but the good of his neighbor."

- Philippians 2:3-4: "Do nothing from rivalry or conceit, but in humility count others more significant than yourselves. Let each of you look not only to his own interests, but also to the interests of others."

- Romans 5:1-2: "We who are strong have an obligation to bear with the failings of the weak, and not to please ourselves. Let each of us please his neighbor for his good, to build him up."

- Romans 2:8: "But for those who are self-seeking and do not obey the truth, but obey unrighteousness, there will be wrath and fury."
- Galatians 5:26: "Let us not become conceited, provoking one another, envying one another."

Truly, we live in a selfish time. Our society is one of self-focus rather than other-focus. People want their own way. They want their own desires to prevail. They want their own views to dominate the conversation, yes, even dominate the society. They only listen to the voices that agree with their own. People are becoming entitled—which is a disease that leads to arrogance.

Many people take countless selfies, so focused on themselves that they hardly notice the needs of the people around them.

It has become a world where people seem to be focused on their own desires, their own outlook, strictly their own well-being, and their own perception of the world.

But here's the good news. There is an antidote to all of this. Just like there is an antidote that will save you from a snake bite, there is an antidote that will save you from trapping yourself into a life of selfishness.

"Focus on God, and focus on the needs of others."

Let us not put the focus on ourselves. Let's focus on how to please God and how to please the people that God has graciously put into our lives.

We already know about the time when Jesus was asked what he thought were the most important teachings in all the Bible. And Jesus gave a direct response that has been echoed for 2000 years.

Matthew 22:36-40:

> Teacher, which is the greatest commandment in the Law?
>
> Jesus replied: "'Love the Lord your God with all your heart and with all your soul and with all your mind.' This is the first and greatest commandment. And the second is like it: 'Love your neighbor as yourself.' All the Law and the Prophets hang on these two commandments."

So, do you want to know how to mess up your life? Do you want to know how to become miserable? Do you want to know how to stay locked up in your own head with your own problems?

The answer is: be selfish. Only think about yourself. It will drive you nuts.

On the other hand, do you want to be delivered from your mental anguish and unnecessary suffering? Do you want to live the restful, fulfilling life that God offers us? Do you want to clean up the messes that you've made in your life?

Then the solution has been provided: stay focused on how to please God. And focus on what you can do to help the people around you.

Wallow in your own self-pity and in your own problems ... and you'll get a miserable, insular life where you feel trapped inside your own head.

But if you want to move on from that ... if you want to get outside of your own head ... if you want to focus on serving other people ... then I assure you ... you will reap the benefits of changing your focus from yourself to 1. God, and 2. To the people around you.

It all begins with repentance. Just like in the journal entry I read to you written by John Williamson, recounting when a younger version of myself knocked on his door that night.

I repented of my sins. I asked the Lord to come into my life. I pledged that I would stop living for myself, and I would start focusing on God. I decided to start actually caring about other people, rather than my own selfish desires, and my own selfish perspective.

I decided to accept the good news of Jesus Christ as a lifestyle, and not just as verbal assent. I decided to turn towards God. With my heart, soul, mind, and strength ... I decided to turn to my Lord and Savior, Jesus Christ.

And shortly thereafter I became a Bible major. I started attending Bible studies every free moment I could do so. I started praying with John Williamson—often deep into the night. My grades skyrocketed and I became a straight A student. I started crafting better goals for myself—that included God and the betterment of people.

Shortly thereafter, I started leading an on-campus devotional on my campus, which gave me the confidence I needed to start ministering. Shortly after that, I was asked to become a professional minister at a country church about an hour from campus—in Edmonson, Texas—with godly farmers as their core membership.

Around that time, I met Sunde, the love of my life. And she supported my ministry then—during my undergraduate years—just as earnestly as she does now—over thirty years later.

My life was a mess. But then I made a decision for Jesus. I decided to follow Him. Just as this book has asked of us. To "follow Jesus." I turned towards Jesus Christ as my master. And that decision made all the difference in my life. The Lord changed me and healed me.

My final charge to you this day is this: Do you want to mess up your life?

Then be selfish. That's all you have to do. If you get extremely selfish ... then you can count on a pretty miserable result. Selfishness breeds all kinds of sins in us: contempt, jealousy, irritability, entitlement, and so forth.

But if you want to experience the freedom that comes in Christ, then remove the focus from yourself, and put it onto God. And when you do that ... God will likely direct you to help someone else.

Maybe you can become what John Williamson was for me, when I knocked on his door late that night at Lubbock Christian University. Way back in 1992.

And maybe ... just maybe ... you can direct some lonesome soul back to the narrow path that Jesus has called us to walk.

20. "Follow Me," Declares the Lord

Let's focus on two words for this final chapter: "*Follow me*." Did you know that Jesus said, "Follow me" around 10 times in the Gospels? Let's look at those passages; it will encourage all of us to follow Him more faithfully.

1. Jesus calls you to become "fishers of people" (Matthew 4:18-22).

> As Jesus was walking beside the Sea of Galilee, he saw two brothers, Simon called Peter and his brother Andrew. They were casting a net into the lake, for they were fishermen. "Come, follow me," Jesus said, "and I will send you out to fish for people." At once, they left their nets and followed him.
>
> Going on from there, he saw two other brothers, James, son of Zebedee and his brother John. They were in a boat with their father Zebedee, preparing their nets. Jesus called them, and immediately they left the boat and their father and followed him.

Throughout this book, Jesus has turned his face towards you, and he has said, "Come, follow me, and I will send you out to fish for people."

Hopefully, this book has motivated you to share the gospel with the people next door, with your coworkers, with your family members who don't know the Lord, and with the people you interact with. When you follow Jesus, you become an evangelist. You become a missionary. Let us go out and bring people to our Master so He can change them into loving, humble, and contagious disciples.

2. You must take up your cross (Matthew 16:24).

> Then Jesus said to his disciples, "Whoever wants to be my disciple must deny themselves and take up their cross and follow me. For whoever wants to save their life will lose it, but whoever loses their life for me will find it."

To follow Jesus, you must sacrifice. You must "take up your cross." The way of Jesus is often the way of suffering. If you decide to be a disciple of Jesus, you must deny yourself. You must "lose your (old) life." And by shedding yourself of your old ways, you will find new life in Christ.

3. You will be blessed with eternal life (Matthew 19:28-29).

> Jesus said to them, "Truly I tell you, at the renewal of all things, when the Son of Man sits on his glorious throne, you who have followed me will also sit on twelve thrones, judging the twelve tribes of Is-

> rael. And everyone who has left houses or brothers or sisters or father or mother or wife or children or fields for my sake will receive a hundred times as much and will inherit eternal life."

Indeed, there is a price to be paid for following Jesus. But "at the renewal of all things," you will be abundantly blessed. If you have suffered for following Jesus, you will receive "a hundred times as much," just as the prophet Job experienced. And, most importantly, you will enter the Kingdom of Heaven, and you will enjoy "eternal life."

4. You must give to the poor (Mark 10:20-22)

> "Teacher," the rich man declared, "all these teachings I have kept since I was a boy."

> Jesus looked at him and loved him. "One thing you lack," he said. "Go, sell everything you have and give to the poor, and you will have treasure in heaven. Then come, follow me."

> At this the man's face fell. He went away sad because he had great wealth.

This is one of the great challenges of the New Testament. Jesus requires us to make a sacrifice. And one of those sacrifices is that we are called to give to the poor. Let us never become so comfortable in our success that we forget to give money and gifts to the poor. Yes, Jesus tells us that we will always have poor people around us, but that is all the more reason to give to them. The man in this story was very rich, and he just couldn't bring himself to give to poor people. I think we've all known people like this. They don't want to help the poor, but unfortunately, they condemn themselves when they refuse to help them.

5. Jesus also has a heart for rich people (Luke 5:26-28)

> After this, Jesus went out and saw a tax collector by the name of Levi sitting at his tax booth. "Follow me," Jesus said to him, and Levi got up, left everything and followed him.

Jesus doesn't just think about the poor. He also calls on the rich. If God blesses you with wealth, then use it for his purposes. Why do you think Jesus called on a rich man to follow him? Maybe that rich man was able to help Jesus's ministry. Let us never despise people who have some measure of wealth. When wealthy people follow Jesus, they can become a huge blessing to the members of the church. They can follow Jesus, too! We must never forget that.

6. Remember, you have found what all people are looking for (John 1:40-41).

> Andrew, Simon Peter's brother, was one of the two who heard what John had said and who had followed Jesus. The first thing Andrew did was to find his brother Simon and tell him, "We have found the Messiah" (that is, the Christ).

The Irish rock band U2 once wrote a song called "I still haven't found what I'm looking for." But you, as a disciple of Jesus, you have found what all men and women are looking for. You have found the Messiah. You don't have to blindly walk around in this life, looking for the next best thing. You can be thankful to God that you have found Him. You have found the truth. There is no longer any reason to try to find your meaning in life. It is right here. You have found the Messiah, the Son of God. Now follow him with all of your heart.

7. God may ask you to go to a distant place (John 1:43-44).

> The next day, Jesus decided to leave for Galilee. Finding Philip, he said to him, "Follow me."
>
> Philip, like Andrew and Peter, was from the town of Bethsaida.

When you follow Jesus, there is no guarantee that you will be comfortable. In fact, there is no guarantee that you will stay where you are. The Lord may call you to a different place. God may call you to a fresh beginning. God may ask you to step out in faith, like He did with Abraham.

A few years ago, I was contacted by a former student of mine, and he was very scared because it seemed to him that God was calling him back to his homeland in the Philippines. He was nervous because he had come to love the United States. But he felt God was calling him back to the land of his birth.

And that is what happens when we follow Jesus, by faith. You may be asked to go to the mission field. You may be asked to do things a little differently. God may tell you that if you follow him, you will have to change your plans.

8. If you follow Jesus, you will walk in the light (John 8:12).

> When Jesus spoke again to the people, he said, "I am the light of the world. Whoever follows me will never walk in darkness, but will have the light of life."

We've all spent some time in the dark. We've wandered around in life, trying to blaze our own trail. And we often find ourselves defeated, maybe kicked to the curb. But when we truly grab hold of Jesus, we are suddenly surrounded by the light of the world. Our world becomes fantastically illuminated.

C.S. Lewis once wrote the following. He said: "I believe in Christianity as I believe that the sun has risen: not only because I see it, but because by it, I see everything else."

Jesus will illuminate everything around you. When you follow Christ, you will notice that everything else is illuminated. With Christ in your life, you will notice all of the blessings around you. You will exit the hopelessness of night, and you will be bathed in His beautiful daylight.

9. Following Jesus may even lead to death (John 21:18-19).

> "Very truly I tell you, when you were younger you dressed yourself and went where you wanted; but

when you are old you will stretch out your hands, and someone else will dress you and lead you where you do not want to go." Jesus said this to indicate the kind of death by which Peter would glorify God. Then he said to him, "Follow me!"

These days, we don't think of Christianity as something that may lead to death. But in the passage we just read, we see Jesus promising Peter that Peter would die a cruel death. In fact, Peter died by being crucified, except upside down. Yet Jesus still commanded Peter to follow Him.

Following Jesus is not something we do as long as it is comfortable. No, following Jesus may indeed be uncomfortable for some of us. And the sooner we understand this, then the sooner we begin to truly walk by faith.

And let us remember that when we follow Jesus unto death, we are truly "glorifying God," even in our suffering.

10. Following Jesus begins today.

I end this book with a call for all of us to follow Jesus beginning now. Don't put it off. Don't think that you will follow him when this or that happens, or when this or that aspect of your life falls into place.

No, Jesus wants you to follow Him today. Don't wait around for something unique to happen. Jesus says, "Follow me." And you and I should do it.

This world is really messed up. People are calling things good that are actually evil according to God. And they are calling evil things good. The world has reversed on us. There is not much righteousness in the world anymore. Things have become confused and crooked, depraved and distrustful. Sometimes it is hard to follow Jesus in a world where we are bombarded by temptations at every turn. Sometimes we just want to throw in the towel and give up.

But Jesus is worth far more than what this world has to offer. Our Lord is the "pearl of great price." He is more precious than silver or gold or cash. He is worthy of your devotion. He is worthy of your allegiance. Trust in Him, and He will give you the true desires of your heart.

Jesus says, "Follow me." You and I both know what that means. Let us surrender our will to His and follow his lead, listening to His voice. He is leading us to the place we need to be. We just have to trust Him.

I hope this book has been helpful to you. More importantly, I hope this book has given you the strength to set your eyes on Jesus Christ as your master, as you follow Him with all of your heart, soul, mind and strength.

About the Author

If you feel generous and have a few minutes, please leave a review online where you purchased this book. It makes a significant difference to the author. Thank you in advance.

Dyron B. Daughrity is the William S. Banowsky Chair in Religion at Pepperdine University in Malibu, California. He is the author of many books and articles in the fields of comparative religion, global Christianity, and world religious history. He has ministered to churches for over 30 years, and is currently the Senior Minister at the Hilltop Community Church of Christ in El Segundo, California. Dyron has been married to Sunde for 30 years and they have four children.

Visit the author's website at:
https://seaver.pepperdine.edu/academics/faculty/dyron-daughrity/

Facebook
https://www.facebook.com/dyron.daughrity

About the Publisher

Sulis International Press publishes select fiction and nonfiction in a variety of genres under four imprints:

- Riversong Books (fiction)
- Sulis Press (general nonfiction)
- Keledei Publications (spirituality)
- Sulis Academic Press (academic works)

For more, visit the website at
https://sulisinternational.com

Subscribe to the newsletter at
https://sulisinternational.com/subscribe/

Follow on social media
https://www.facebook.com/SulisInternational
https://twitter.com/Sulis_Intl
https://www.pinterest.com/Sulis_Intl/
https://www.instagram.com/sulis_international/

www.ingramcontent.com/pod-product-compliance
Lightning Source LLC
Chambersburg PA
CBHW032116090426
42743CB00007B/377